SESSIONS WITH EZRA & NEHEMIAH

Smyth & Helwys Publishing, Inc.
6316 Peake Road
Macon, Georgia 31210-3960
1-800-747-3016
© 2016 by Randy Shepley

Library of Congress Cataloging-in-Publication Data

Names: Shepley, Randy, author.
Title: Sessions with Ezra-Nehemiah : new beginnings with God / by Randy
Shepley.
Description: Macon : Smyth & Helwys, 2016. | Includes bibliographical
references.
Identifiers: LCCN 2016003388 | ISBN 9781573128667 (pbk. : alk. paper)
Subjects: LCSH: Bible. Ezra--Textbooks. | Bible. Nehemiah--Textbooks.
Classification: LCC BS1355.55 .S54 2016 | DDC 222/.707--dc23
LC record available at http://lccn.loc.gov/2016003388

Sessions *with* Ezra & Nehemiah

New Beginnings
with *God*

Randy Shepley

SMYTH&HELWYS
PUBLISHING, INCORPORATED   MACON, GEORGIA

Also by Randy Shepley

Going for the Jugular
(co-authored with Walter B. Shurden)

To my wife, Alice.
Her love for Jesus and the Bible is what first attracted me to her.
The joy of doing our lives together with God is
more remarkable than I ever imagined.

Acknowledgments

Any book is both a labor of love and angst. I want to thank everyone who has suffered with me as I have lived in the states of love, angst, and everywhere in between while wrestling with Ezra and Nehemiah. I especially want to thank my wife, Alice, and my children, James, Samuel, and Elizabeth. They have put up with books and commentaries littered across the floor and also with my moods as I have tried to find the correct facts, stories, and phrases. I love them more than I can convey, and their patience and encouragement during this writing is a deeply treasured gift. I also want to thank my mom and dad for their continued focus on my spiritual formation. They have never given up on seeing Christ formed in me.

I also want to thank the churches where I have served over the years. In each place, the stories of Ezra and Nehemiah have resonated and offered guidance to our journeys. Now, as a relatively new pastor at the First Baptist Church, Newport News, Virginia, I am looking forward to sharing the stories of Ezra and Nehemiah again and allowing the Holy Spirit to shape us with their truth. I want to thank Michael McCullar and Keith Gammons for inviting me to write part of the Sessions series. This study would not be possible without their gracious invitation.

Finally, I want to thank my childhood pastor and mentor, William L. Self, who baptized me, received me as I dedicated my life to "vocational Christian service," encouraged me to go to Mercer University and the Candler School of Theology, and listened and gave wise counsel during all the days of my ministry. Bill has now gone to live with the Lord he loved and proclaimed with his entire life, but he has left behind a profound legacy of faith. I am indebted to him and so many others who have counseled and guided me along the journey.

Table of Contents

Introduction ix

Session 1 1
God's Deliverance in Unexpected Places
Ezra 1:1-11

Session 2 11
Starting Over
Ezra 3:6

Session 3 21
Hitting the Wall
Ezra 4

Session 4 31
From Inertia to Engagement
Ezra 5:1-5; 6:1-5, 13-22

Session 5 41
The Return of the Law
Ezra 7:6-10, 13-17, 25-26

Session 6 51
An Unrelenting Burden
Nehemiah 1

Session 7 61
Making a Plea . . . Crafting a Plan
Nehemiah 2

Session 8 71
Overcoming Obstacles, Outlasting Critics
Nehemiah 4

Session 9 81
Conviction, Celebration, and Worship
Nehemiah 8

Session 10 91
Confession and Covenant
Nehemiah 9

Notes 101

Works Cited 103

Introduction

Opening Words

The Old Testament books of Ezra and Nehemiah are inseparably joined in terms of their purpose, themes, and characters. While the two books exist as separate writings in the biblical canon, they were originally one work in the early Jewish traditions. Ezra-Nehemiah relays the story and theological themes associated with the return from exile of the people of Israel. The return of the exiles began in 538 BC with the edict of King Cyrus of Persia. Cyrus gave official permission for the Jewish exiles to return to Jerusalem, rebuild the temple, and reestablish the city. According to primary sources uncovered by archaeologists and biblical scholars, Cyrus pursued a policy of restoration regarding captured cities in highly strategic locations. So Cyrus gave the people permission to relocate to their home in Jerusalem, and his treasury provided the funds for rebuilding the temple.

The significance of the return of the exiles cannot be overstated. In 587 BC, the Babylonian king Nebuchadnezzar overran Jerusalem. The siege and destruction of the city were especially brutal. The city wall was torn down, the temple decimated, and the royal palace burned. Furthermore, Zedekiah, the king of Judah, watched as the Babylonian army executed his sons and the nobles of Jerusalem. After witnessing the executions, Zedekiah was blinded and led off in chains to Babylon. Along with the king, almost the entire population of Jerusalem was taken into exile. Nebuchadnezzar only left behind the poorest city dwellers. The defeat was catastrophic and complete.

Jeremiah, one of the prophets of the Lord present at the fall of Jerusalem, made it clear to the people their defeat was not a result of poor strategy or an ill-equipped military. Instead, the defeat of Judah was rooted in the sin of the people. The people of God had defied their covenantal commitment to God through many generations. The kings of the people "did evil in the eyes of the LORD" and refused to lead the people into lives of worship and holiness to God. God cried out to the people through the prophets and acts of deliverance, but the people continually turned away. So God spoke words of judgment through the prophet Jeremiah:

Thus says the LORD:
Stand at the crossroads, and look,
        and ask for the ancient paths,
where the good way lies; and walk in it,
        and find rest for your souls.
But they said, "We will not walk in it."

Also I raised up sentinels for you:
        "Give heed to the sound of the trumpet!"
But they said, "We will not give heed."

Therefore hear, O nations,
        and know, O congregation, what will happen to them.

Hear, O earth; I am going to bring disaster on this people,
        the fruit of their schemes,
because they have not given heed to my words;
        and as for my teaching, they have rejected it. (Jer 6:16-19)

The story of the people of Judah, then, is about a people who committed to a covenant relationship with God under the leadership of Moses, and then rejected that covenant through ongoing disobedience to God. This covenant dismissal culminated in the destruction of Jerusalem at the hands of the Babylonian Empire. Ezra and Nehemiah, then, tell the story of the people of Israel as they embrace a new start in Jerusalem and a restoration of their covenant relationship with God. Ezra and Nehemiah tell the good news of new beginnings, even when the new beginnings bring danger, uncertainty, disagreement, and discouragement.

Why Study Ezra and Nehemiah?

Ezra and Nehemiah rarely make it into sermon rotations or the spiritual discipline patterns of individual Jesus followers. In addition, Ezra and Nehemiah are not standard material in the scope and sequence of most Sunday school curricular resources. Therefore, it is likely that most small group and Sunday school class members will know little about the stories contained in these writings. In addition, the background story of Judah's exile is unfamiliar and confusing to most churchgoers. Finally, the chronology of the books is puzzling, adding to their apparent inaccessibility to all but serious Old Testament scholars.

For those who undertake the adventure of studying Ezra-Nehemiah, however, there are immeasurable opportunities for learning and faith development. The rich theological themes of Ezra-Nehemiah address many critical questions current to cultural and theological conversation today.

First, Ezra and Nehemiah teach the process of grace and redemption. The book of Ezra begins with the proclamation of King Cyrus that gives permission to the Jewish people to return to Jerusalem. This is a salvific moment for the people. The writer of Ezra states that the Lord "moved the heart of Cyrus king of Persia" (Ezra 1:1). In Isaiah 45:1, the author of Second Isaiah names Cyrus as a messiah, an anointed one of God, because his proclamation delivers God's people from exile. The command of Cyrus is the signal that God is saving and redeeming God's people out of exile, but it is not the sign of unbridled prosperity. Instead, the exiles who return to Jerusalem face difficulty, opposition, and a scarcity of resources. Experiencing the salvation of the Lord does not secure prosperity, healing, or easy living. Instead, God's grace and redemption guarantee God's presence and provision whether life is prosperous or painful. The experience of the exiles reinforces truths about process and journey related to grace and redemption.

Second, Ezra and Nehemiah portray how a religious group embodies their faith as a minority movement in a larger, pluralistic culture. The returning exiles arrive in Jerusalem to an environment where they are surrounded by neighbors who do not share their national or religious beliefs. In fact, there is mistrust for the Jewish people who have returned. How will the returning exiles live out their covenant with God in a culture where their religious expression is the minority view? This was not only a critical question for the Jewish people returning from exile; it also represents one of the critical questions of American Christianity. Since we live in a post-Christendom era, where many Americans no longer know the basic arc of the biblical story, followers of Jesus struggle to articulate faith in a culture where Christianity is unknown, mistrusted, misunderstood, and even dismissed. We can learn much about living in our current spiritual context from the lessons of Ezra and Nehemiah.

Third, Ezra and Nehemiah wrestle with how ministers and lay leaders lead people of faith to develop courage and holiness. Spiritual leadership is a critical theme in Ezra and Nehemiah. Ezra is called by King Artaxerxes of Persia to lead the people of Jerusalem along the path of spiritual renewal. How does a pastor, Sunday school teacher, or deacon serve as a catalyst for spiritual renewal in the church? Likewise, Nehemiah is charged to lead the people in rebuilding the walls of Jerusalem, a task left undone for decades due to opposition, despair, and a lack of organization. The leadership examples of Ezra and Nehemiah offer rich insights for all who struggle to lead people forward in faith and community development.

Fourth, the story of Ezra and Nehemiah gives encouragement to churches who struggle with the nostalgia of their past even as they move forward into their future. The dream of the returning exiles involves Jerusalem returning to world prominence and eventually living under the leadership of its own king, answerable only to God. Unfortunately, the returning exiles and their descendants never see a nation as prosperous or significant on the world stage as the Israel of the Davidic kingdom. Even the victories they accomplish pale when compared to the former glories of the nation of Israel. In the present, so many churches are smaller and less influential than they were at the height of American Christendom. How do people of faith live as faithful bands of believers when the days of big attendance, big budgets, and full nurseries have vanished? If we listen, the books of Ezra and Nehemiah will offer some clues.

Finally, Ezra and Nehemiah tell the story of how a people move from disordered chaos to spiritual community. As mentioned in the paragraph above, the people returned to find that what they most wanted—a faith community and a healthy city—was not yet possible. The returning exiles and their descendants strive to create a community in covenant relationship with God in the midst of unfulfilled promises. They live in the tension between the work they imagine God will do in Israel and the work they see God doing that does not match their expectations. They must learn to see God do marvelous works even amid chaos.

Authorship and Chronology

Before moving on to the Bible study sessions, it is necessary to comment on the questions of authorship and chronology regarding Ezra and Nehemiah. Both of these questions have produced numerous pages of scholarly debate over the years. At present, there are varying levels of consensus related to issues of the authorship and chronology of Ezra and Nehemiah.

There is general agreement among scholars that Ezra-Nehemiah is the continuation of the story told in 1 and 2 Chronicles. Many scholars also consider Chronicles and Ezra-Nehemiah the work of the same author. Traditionally, Ezra was believed to be the author of these works, but present scholarship suggests that 1 and 2 Chronicles and Ezra-Nehemiah were penned by the "Chronicler," an anonymous individual who compiled these works to tell the story of Israel and Judah's betrayal of covenant, and God's resulting judgment. There is disagreement about whether the same author actually wrote 1 and 2 Chronicles and Ezra-Nehemiah, but it is generally held that Ezra was not the author and Ezra-Nehemiah was written as a continuation of the Chronicler perspective.

The chronology present within Ezra-Nehemiah is even murkier than its authorship. When one reads Ezra and Nehemiah through in one sitting, it is a struggle to determine when Ezra and Nehemiah arrived in Jerusalem, how connected the two were with one another, and how many years are actually covered by the events of Ezra-Nehemiah. The discussions among scholars and commentaries regarding chronology issues in Ezra-Nehemiah run the gamut: Is it possible that Nehemiah arrived in Jerusalem before Ezra, even though the traditional view has Ezra arriving in the seventh year of Artaxerxes I and Nehemiah arriving in the twenty-first year of Artaxerxes I? Is it possible that Ezra arrived during the reign of Artaxerxes II?

For scholars, these questions are interesting, but for the layperson reading the text, they are confusing. In order to minimize confusion, this study will follow the traditional interpretation of Ezra arriving in Jerusalem first (458 BC), with Nehemiah arriving fourteen years later for his first gubernatorial appointment. Even with this interpretive stance, the chronology of the text is difficult to decipher. The truth, however, is that one can draw deep wisdom for faithful living from Ezra-Nehemiah even with hazy clarity regarding its chronology. Ezra-Nehemiah is not striving for precise record keeping; rather, it reveals the truth of salvation history—that God works in history to redeem God's people even from exile.

God's Deliverance in Unexpected Places

Central Text: Ezra 1:1-11
Background Text: Ezra 1-2

In 1990, Atlantans witnessed a most remarkable and unexpected event. After three and a half years of lobbying, publicizing, and politicking, the International Olympic Committee announced on September 18, 1990, that the city of Atlanta would host the Summer Olympics in 1996. As a native Atlantan, the news overwhelmed me with equal parts of disbelief and exultation. I am proud of my home city, and yet the announcement was surreal. How could Atlanta win a competition between Athens, Greece; Toronto, Canada; and Melbourne, Australia?[1] The influence of Andrew Young and the superiority of Atlanta's existing infrastructure were major reasons for Atlanta's victory, but actually winning the bid seemed so improbable. It was a profound upset.

Atlantans were proud. We celebrated winning the position of host for the Olympic games as if our Atlanta Falcons had won the Super Bowl (which, as of this writing, still has not happened). The announcement stoked a pride in our city that was nonexistent only hours before the announcement. Now more than ever, Atlanta was on the map, and we stood poised, ready to reap the economic rewards of the coming Olympics.

The truth, however, was that we had not won a victory. Instead, Atlanta was granted the responsibility to host the Olympic games. On the day and immediate weeks after the announcement, celebration and pride carried Atlantans through their routines. Soon, however, Atlantans beyond the organizing committee began to realize the work and cost involved in hosting the summer games. Venues were built, including a new Olympic stadium, at tremendous cost. Some of these venues would struggle to find uses after the games departed, essentially relegated to forgotten complexes of varying sustainability. Neighborhoods were moved in order to build housing for athletes, public housing projects were demolished, conversations were held about how to help the people who were displaced, and, of course, everything cost more than was set aside.

In the end, the reaction of the nation and the world to the Atlanta Olympics was, at best, mixed. The bombing in Centennial Olympic Park during the games was a tragic occurrence that shifted the focus of the games. Others simply shared their opinions that Atlanta was not up to the Olympic challenge, particularly in the area of transportation. In retrospect, Atlanta's Olympics faced an insurmountable set of presumptions. Georgia State University marketing professor Ken Barnhardt commented, "People had very unrealistic expectations of what the Olympics could do . . . it was not practical to count on a long-term economic boost."[2] The joy of Atlanta's receiving the games did not measure up to the experience of the Olympics, even though the games themselves brought positive economic impact and energy into the city.

Like the one on September 28, 1990, in Atlanta, Georgia, the book of Ezra begins with a stunning and unexpected announcement. After almost fifty years in exile (although some members of the community had spent nearly sixty years in exile after Nebuchadnezzar's first deportation of the people of Judah), the Jewish people are allowed to return to Jerusalem. The Edict of King Cyrus must have inspired initial celebration. The people had waited decades for this deliverance, perhaps even losing hope that it would happen at all. The initial euphoria, however, must have given way to trepidation and uncertainty. Exilic living was not pain free, but the people were allowed to build their own homes (Jer 29:5 and Ezek 8:1), marry, earn a living as a part of the community, and, in essence, carve a life out of the desperation of deportation. Some of the exiles like Daniel achieved high levels of prominence in Babylonian and later Persian society. While the situation was not idyllic, it is reasonable to assume that many of the exiles made a new life and new families for themselves in the Babylonian culture. The opportunity to return to their homeland was welcomed and celebrated, but it also brought anxiety. How would the Jewish community in exile respond to the decree of Cyrus?

The motivation behind Cyrus's decree deserves attention. According to the so-called Cyrus Cylinder, which was a building piece covered with inscriptions unearthed in Babylon, the policy of Cyrus's rule was to return the peoples of Babylon to their native lands.

In addition, the Persian Empire would fund the rebuilding costs of places of worship for these peoples. So multiple people groups—including the Jewish people—in areas under Persian control were allowed to return to their homelands.

Why would Cyrus issue an edict allowing so many exiled peoples to return to their native lands? The answer conveyed a reversal in political strategy from the Babylonian Empire. While the Babylonian Empire enforced obedience and loyalty through deportation and subjugation, Cyrus chose to inspire allegiance through granting a measured amount of freedom and autonomy. The returning exiles would have responsibility and opportunity, although they would still live under the rule of Persia. The reasoning behind this approach was that native persons on their native soil would exercise a higher level of care and initiative in rebuilding their communities, and they would live out their loyalty to Persia not only out of fear but also out of appreciation.

The writer of Ezra, however, neglects to mention the unilateral nature of the Persian policy of exile resettlement. In fact, the author issues a profound claim of faith regarding the Edict of Cyrus: "the LORD stirred up the spirit of King Cyrus of Persia so that he sent a herald throughout all his kingdom" (Ezra 1:1). In other words, the author insists that the Edict of King Cyrus was not merely a politically motivated strategy for ordered resettlement designed to promote loyalty and stability in the Persian Empire. Instead, it was an act of God, who was keeping God's promise to deliver the Jewish people out of exile and back to the land God gave them as a part of the covenants with Abraham and Moses. For the author of Ezra, the action of Cyrus is nothing short of God's fulfillment of the words spoken by Jeremiah:

> For thus says the LORD: Only when Babylon's seventy years are completed will I visit you, and I will fulfill to you my promise and bring you back to this place. For surely I know the plans I have for you, says the LORD, plans for your welfare and not for harm, to give you a future with hope. Then when you call upon me and come and pray to me, I will hear you. When you search for me, you will find me; if you seek me with all your heart, I will let you find me, says the LORD, and I will restore your fortunes and gather you from all the nations and all the places where I have driven you, says the LORD, and I will bring you back to the place from which I sent you into exile. (Jer 29:10-14)

How can one justify the approach of the author of Ezra that attributes the Edict of Cyrus to the action of God's Spirit without mentioning the underlying political realities? The writer of Ezra sees the action of Cyrus as the work of God even in the midst of Persian culture and policies. The author is not attempting to document the political realities of the return of the exiles. Instead, he sees the hand of God at work in the actions of Cyrus and interprets the edict as the deliverance activity of God, even though the popular culture of the Persian empire would see Cyrus's actions only as a reversal of prior Babylonian policy regarding the exiles. Cyrus is designated as the anointed one (literally, messiah) of God in Isaiah 45:1, not because he willingly engages in God's purposes but because God uses his actions to accomplish the redemption of God's people.

One of the hallmarks of a maturing Christian faith is to see in one's life, relationships, and culture the activity of the Spirit of God. The story we read in Ezra and Nehemiah, and indeed all through the Old Testament, is the story of God working through regular people and circumstances to accomplish God's work of redemption in Jesus Christ. Followers of Jesus look at the circumstances of their world, the situations in their offices, the relationships in their neighborhoods, the concerns of their communities, and the actions of their churches through the question, "Where do we see the Spirit of God at work?" We are convinced through the testimony of Scripture, prayer, and community with other believers that our world is not left in free-falling chaos but that God is on mission in creation, even in the midst of evil, disorder, and unexplainable circumstances. God is actively at work for the sake of the redemption of all creation, and followers of Jesus have the opportunity to live within God's incarnational mission. In fact, God uses people outside the church, even people like Cyrus who have no connection to God at all, to accomplish God's mission. The writer of Ezra recognizes the redemptive activity of God in the actions of Cyrus and shares with the people of Judah that God has not forgotten them. Indeed, even the leader of the entire empire is subject to God's purposes and mission.

Obviously, King Cyrus did not see himself as the one used by God to deliver the Jewish people. As noted above, the author of Ezra sees the hand of God behind the actions of Cyrus and therefore turns the recounting of Cyrus's work into confessional history. The people of Israel learn to read history through the eyes of God's promises and their covenant with God, even if the actors within the historical drama do not see or ascribe to God's activity. It is vital for followers of Jesus to recognize and interpret the work of God's Holy Spirit in their lives, communities, and cultures. The truth, however, is that Christ-followers can make mistakes about where God is working. It is even possible for Christians to manipulate the truths of Scripture to endorse actions, beliefs, and attitudes that are not works of the Holy Spirit. How, then, does one know that what is claimed as the work of God is actually God?

In the case of the people of Israel, the truth of God's work in history was discerned through the community of faith. Over the generations, the people told and tested the stories of God. Also, as they shared the stories of God's faithfulness in the Exodus-Sinai experience and during the days of David, and even as they passed along the damning and convicting words of the prophets, they experienced inside their hearts the truth of God and confirmed it within their group. In fact, they found that the truth of God working through God's covenant with Israel still held firm even after decades of exile. The people learned that God was at work in Cyrus because they had passed along stories of how God previously worked through the external activities and persons of their world, including God triumphing over and working through the mighty pharaoh of Egypt. Likewise, when we hear claims of God at work in the world, we test these claims alongside the stories of Scripture and the prayers and conversation of the faith community.

Sometimes, however, it takes churches, church people, and church leaders a long while to hear and see how God is at work in the world. The Bible and church history are riddled with stories of prophetic voices that were ignored or in many cases silenced even when they speak the truth. So, when we hear people claiming to see God at work in the world, we must listen with humility so we will not miss what God is doing. We also must be careful and humble in proclaiming where we see God at work. If we are not careful, we will become people who "cry wolf" about God's activity, and no one will listen to us. Words about God's work in the world are not prophetic because we certify their prophetic authenticity; rather, the Holy Spirit gives and reveals prophetic speech. Therefore, humility and discernment are critical practices for ascertaining where and how God is at work in the world.

In reading Ezra 1, we must not ignore the purpose the author of Ezra sees in Cyrus's declaration to the Jewish people. In verse 2, Cyrus proclaims that God has appointed him "to build a temple for him at Jerusalem in Judah." The historical parallels in Cyrus's proclamation are hard to miss. First, King Cyrus releases the Jewish people, "letting them go" back to the land of their ancestors, in effect mirroring the original exodus event where Pharaoh was compelled by the hand of God to release the Israelites from slavery. Of course, there are many differences between the original exodus and the return from exile, but the critical similarity for the Jewish nation is that God acts on behalf of Israel by compelling the ruler of an empire to release God's people.

Second, King Cyrus sends the people back to Jerusalem with the specific charge to build a temple to God. One of the deepest disappointments regarding the defeat of Jerusalem in 587 was the destruction of the temple, which signaled a dramatic shift in the faith of the nation of Judah. The defeat of Judah by Babylon indicated, at least in the cultural understanding of the time, that Babylon's gods were superior to the God of Judah. In addition, the people considered the temple God's dwelling place. If the temple was destroyed, did that mean God left them? Did it mean God was homeless and fully overpowered? Faith questions like these, and the doubts connected with them, followed the people of Judah into exile. While in exile, some of the people stopped following God altogether and adopted the religious practices of the Babylonians. Others saw following God as part of their civil religion as a people, but religious practice and spiritual discipline were not part of their lives. There was, however, a remnant of people who prayed, told the stories of God, and looked for the deliverance of God promised by the prophets. Hearing that they were released to return to Jerusalem and to rebuild the temple of the Lord was not merely news of returning home to the faithful remnant. For them, it was proof that God had not forgotten them, that God was still working in history on their behalf, and that God wanted to restore a covenant relationship with them. After all, a new temple meant a fresh start.

Followers of Jesus can take two profound lessons from Ezra 1:1-11. First, we can learn to see all of our lives as moments and places where God is at work. In fact, it is often when we are outside the church structures and programs that we discern the call and activity of God. Second, when we experience great moments of victory and deliverance in our lives, we often find ourselves immediately confronted by challenges, increased responsibilities, and even opposition. This was certainly the case for the Atlanta Olympic organizing committee after earning the right to host the 1996 Olympic Games. As we will see in session 2, it was certainly true that the joy of the returning exiles would give way to hard work, opposition, and discouragement. So, when we enjoy moments of significant deliverance or victory, we must prepare ourselves for the challenges that lie ahead. God's deliverance paves the way for greater responsibility and covenant partnership for God's people.

1. How much experience do you have reading the book of Ezra? What are you hoping to learn from this little-known treasure of the Bible?

_____
_____
_____
_____
_____

2. Share a time when you experienced a significant victory in your life.

_____
_____
_____
_____
_____

3. How was God an active part in the victory you described in question 2?

_____
_____
_____
_____
_____

4. Describe a time when a person who was not a follower of Jesus made a significant personal/spiritual impact on your life.

_____

_____

_____

_____

_____

5. How do you discern where God is at work in your church and in your community?

_____

_____

_____

_____

_____

6. Where do you see the Spirit of God at work in your church family?

_____

_____

_____

_____

_____

7. Where do you see God at work in your community?

_____

_____

_____

_____

8. Is it hard for you to accept that God used the pagan King Cyrus (even referring to him as a messiah!) to deliver God's people? Why or why not?

_____

_____

_____

_____

_____

9. Is it difficult for you to see God at work in your community outside the church or other Christian organizations? Why or why not?

_____

_____

_____

_____

_____

10. Share a time when you experienced a great victory in your life followed by a prolonged period of greater responsibility, stress, or opposition.

_____

_____

_____

_____

_____

11. As you look across the story of your life, when have you felt closest to God? When have you felt most distant from God?

_____

_____

_____

_____

_____

Starting Over

Central Text: Ezra 3:6
Background Text: Ezra 3

When I write a sermon, article, paper, or book, I often end up in a local restaurant. I enjoy the talking, background noise, and sweet tea I find when I write in a restaurant setting. Even more, I look forward to unexpected conversations with wait staff, friends, and other restaurant patrons. In order to begin writing this session, therefore, I decided to go to one of my favorite local places less than a mile from my home.

As I entered the restaurant, I ran into a husband and wife who are members of our church, and we began talking and laughing together. When I asked what they had done during the day, the husband turned reflective. As it happened, he was at his office packing boxes. His retirement was only a couple of weeks away, so he was sorting through the items he had acquired over his time at the company. He had a lot of work to do because he had served this particular company for thirty-one years, and he was in the same office for nearly that entire time. As I listened, it dawned on me how challenging this executive's task was. He was looking forward to specific adventures and opportunities awaiting him in retirement. He was content and happy with his career accomplishments and with the way he was finishing this stage of his life. Even so, there was much change to face, and many tasks—mental, physical, emotional, and spiritual—to handle. He faced packing up books, photographs, and other office mementos. He faced many hours of processing the memories of his vocational experience and pondering how God wanted him to invest his considerable gifts for the future. When one has served in leadership at the same company for thirty-one years, one does not simply walk away. There are many tasks connected with moving on to the next stage, and many of these tasks require continuing energy, effort, and emotion.

The retirement of my friend made me think of the situation of the Jewish exiles described in the opening chapters of Ezra. In chapter 1, the Jewish exiles celebrated their Divine deliverance through the actions of King Cyrus. Now, however, in chapters 2 and 3, the exiles realize how much work is involved in returning to Jerusalem. The people of Israel have lived in Babylon for nearly fifty years, and some members of the Jewish people were present in Babylon even longer. They had acquired friendships, businesses, homes, and stuff! Anyone who has ever moved knows how difficult it is to sort through all the items in preparation for the relocation. Certainly, this was part of the experience for all the Jewish people who decided to return to Jerusalem.

Of course, not every person connected with the Jewish exile decided to return home. Certainly, many second-generation Jews, the ones who had never felt the soil of the promised land beneath their feet, chose to remain in Babylon. When you have connections, familiar routines, and comfort, why would you choose to return to a desolate land mired in physical and economic ruin? Even though Cyrus gave permission for the Jewish people to return, this does not mean all or even most of them would attempt the journey. Choosing to go back to Jerusalem was a remarkable act of faith all its own.

According to Ezra 2:64, a total of 42,360 people connected with exiled families, excluding servants, returned to Jerusalem. Interestingly enough, this sum is more than the numbers of the specific groupings listed in Ezra 2, but it is hard to imagine that someone was counting every single person carefully. The group was getting ready to move, with all the hassles and issues moving entails. The attempt to write down as many people as possible, however, is important. Like the list of alumni from a college or other institution, inclusion on the list in Ezra 2 meant you had accomplished something significant. Inclusion on the list of returning exiles meant you were one who had lived in Babylon and journeyed back to Jerusalem in order to honor and follow the God who delivered you not only from the bondage of Egypt but also from the bondage of exile. The list of returning exiles is a list of people who decided to believe and reenact their faith in a new era. Their names represent a people who refused to give up and a God who would not let them go.

Ezra offers no information about the journey to Jerusalem, but we can imagine it was difficult and demoralizing. Moving 42,360 people over hundreds of miles across the wilderness, all of them carrying their belongings, is not an easy task, even for a people with a nomadic heritage and culture. When they arrive in Jerusalem, the people are released to their own towns and areas of origin for seven months. One can imagine that during these months, people set up their homes, planted crops, and made provisions for how they would survive in their new surroundings.

After seven months, all of the returnees gathered in Jerusalem. The purpose of their gathering was spiritual. In their presence, the priests began to build the altar of the Lord. Once the altar was constructed, the priests reestablished the patterns and practices of sacrifice that were part of the worship initiated through God's covenant with Moses.

The priests not only reintroduced the sacrifices of the Law to the people but also led them in following the festival commands of God. The people began to celebrate the Feast of Tabernacles. This feast is described in Leviticus 23:33-43. It is a feast that celebrates the provision of God through the productivity of the soil and, more important, celebrates the deliverance of the people of Israel from slavery in Egypt. To commemorate the Feast of Tabernacles, the people lived for seven days in small booths they constructed. The booths reminded the people of the small shelters they had built during the forty-year exodus journey from Egypt to Canaan. One can imagine that the Feast of Tabernacles was especially meaningful to the returning exiles since they had only recently made the long trek from Babylon to Jerusalem, celebrating God's deliverance from exile along the way.

So the Jewish exiles arrived in Jerusalem, prepared their residences and fields, and then came together to initiate practices of corporate worship in gratitude for God's deliverance. All is not well, however, in the areas surrounding Jerusalem. Ezra 3:3 tells us the returnees were afraid of the people living around them. To their credit, the Jewish people overcame fear of their neighbors and moved forward with their worship practices. Both the opposition of their neighbors and the fear of the Jewish people, however, foreshadow important developments in the writing of Ezra and Nehemiah. The initial fear of the returning exiles reminds us of the precarious nature of the foothold the Jewish people fashion in Jerusalem. People groups who are not pleased with their return surround them. Even though the exiles enjoy the support of King Cyrus, Cyrus and his armies are hundreds of miles away. If the people of God are going to survive and return to worshiping the One who delivered them, they will have to overcome their fear and move forward in the face of opposition.

Before moving on to the portion of Ezra 3 where the people begin building the temple foundation, it is important to consider the question of spiritual rhythms. As we have noted, the people spent their first seven months in Jerusalem establishing their home routines and practices for provision. While we know little about the specifics of these seven months, it is reasonable to assume that regular routines for chores, eating, and shelter were enacted for the physical welfare of each family unit. When the whole returning population gathered in Jerusalem after seven months, the people reestablished their rhythms of covenant worship, including the patterns of sacrifice dictated by the Law and the rhythm of festival celebration dictated in Leviticus 23. Both the physical routines and the corporate worship routines of the people are cemented during the initial seven-month period.

In addition, however, the offering rituals were reestablished, allowing the people to practice personal and family habits of devotion. While the faith practice of the Jewish people was community rather than individually focused, individuals and families had roles to play in their own spiritual development. Because of this, the priests and Levites quickly established the system for freewill offerings so individuals and families could bring sacrifices to the temple as the Law and their own introspection demanded. It was critical for corporate worship to function so that people could engage and develop their own spiritual rhythms and, in doing so, recognize and affirm that God was indeed present with them. Recommitting to faith practices, even after the years of exile, reinvests the returning exiles in the covenant faith of their ancestors and helps them reconnect with the God who delivered them and longed to inaugurate a new covenant relationship with them.

After a season of upheaval, distraction, or even tragedy, it is often meaningful for people to develop a pattern of spiritual practices that help them move forward into a new season of life. These practices include prayer, Scripture reading, solitude, silence, and any others of the ancient spiritual habits (also known as spiritual disciplines) that faithful followers of Jesus have used for centuries to connect with God. Of course, spiritual disciplines are not indicators of spiritual health or spiritual maturity in and of themselves. Instead, these disciplines are natural rhythms that help place a person in a position that is attentive to God. During times of transition, our routines are fractured and discombobulated. As normalcy returns, initiating new spiritual rhythms that create space to listen for God can hasten the advent of healing, contentment, and peace. As our lives change, our spiritual practices, rhythms, and pace must change too, even though our habits like public worship, prayer, and Scripture reading may appear the same as always. With the reinstitution of temple worship, the patterns of connecting with God changed for the people from how they worshiped in Babylon. When our life routines face transitions, we must reevaluate our spiritual practices so that we are prepared to listen for the Spirit of God.

In Ezra 3:8-9, the author describes the beginning of the temple reconstruction project. As noted in session 1 above, rebuilding the temple and reinstituting worship of God were the reasons Cyrus authorized the people to return home. So, after caring for their basic needs and beginning the process of rebuilding the rhythms of corporate and personal worship, the people focused on temple construction. The former temple was demolished by the troops of King Nebuchadnezzar during the siege and destruction of Jerusalem in 587 BC. The people, therefore, had to begin with laying the foundation of the temple.

There is a significant parenthetical expression in verse 8 in the NIV: "(the priests and the Levites and all who had returned from captivity to Jerusalem) began the work." The writer of Ezra specifies that every person who returned to Jerusalem worked on the temple construction project. This is significant. The responsibility of living in covenant with the God who delivered them from Egypt and exile belonged to every member of the community, not simply to the priests and the Levites. Everyone worked to see the temple restored. No exceptions.

This is very different from congregations today. In my own Baptist tradition, churches often have many people who attend worship services and do little else to support the church during the week or, even more important, regularly and specifically love and pray for the neighbors in their community, office, and other spheres of influence. Inadvertently, we have made two profound errors in judgment: (1) we have ceded the responsibility for worship, pastoral care, and evangelism to the clergy and certain lay leaders, and (2) we have decided that the most important tasks for the clergy and lay leaders center on church institution work. Baptists and other Christian denominations move forward with few people engaged in the work of maintaining the church schedule and programming, while everyone neglects the work of the kingdom of God outside the walls.

As a pastor, I know how hard it is to get everyone in a congregation to attend regularly, much less get everyone to work on an idea that truly benefits the kingdom of God in our community. The leadership and initiative shown by the players in this temple foundation-building project is impressive. What would it take in the churches of American culture to gain this level of buy-in and participation in a true kingdom endeavor? It would involve an understanding of church membership where all members own real spiritual responsibility, and clergy and congregational leadership cast the vision of the kingdom of God in such a compelling fashion that people inside and outside the church are drawn to participation. What a wonderful vision: all people of a congregation and even people outside the congregation participating together in building a tutoring ministry, a park for the community, an after-school gathering place, or any other number of ideas that invite leaders and participants toward the kingdom of God. Imagine a vision of God's presence and work so powerful that everyone works for it. Everyone.

When the foundation of the temple was completed, the people held a ceremony of dedication. The ceremony followed the rules of King David for temple worship. The people sang words of deep faith, "He is good and his love toward Israel endures forever," a paraphrase of the words found in Psalm 118:1. What a meaningful statement of faith for the people of Israel to sing about God's love that endures forever. They celebrate God giving them the strength to endure the exile, to survive the journey home, and to rebuild the temple foundation. In this service of worship, the people recognize and confess that God, even in Babylon, was preparing for their deliverance. The shouts of joy from the temple foundations are the sound of a people who have experienced the restoration not only of their land but also of their voice of faith. All the emotion of their deliverance and God's provision comes forth in mighty shouts and songs of faith.

All, however, is not joy on this day of victory. Amid the shouts of joy and songs of praise, there is another sound: weeping. Why are the people sad? Many in their number remember the grandness of the former temple. They recall its size, splendor, and the power that God had bestowed on their former nation. Perhaps the thought crosses their minds that if they had remained obedient to God's covenant commands, Jerusalem would not have faced destruction and they would never have endured the exile. Even in the midst of victory and celebration, many in the nation notice that the temple is nowhere near as grand and great as it once was, just like their nation itself. The glaring juxtaposition between the temple of the past and the foundation of the present reminds the people of how far they have fallen, and they respond with tears, even while celebrating.

Most of us know the irony of the joy of celebration mingling with tears of grief. A man in a congregation I served as pastor was in the first wave of soldiers who landed on Omaha beach during the D-Day invasion. A couple of years ago, I saw him honored by the French government for the role he played in liberating their nation from the occupation of Nazi Germany. There was such profound celebration, and yet this man, like so many others, lost dear friends on that day. How can people like him remember such a momentous victory without deep sadness?

When a loved one dies, there is grief and sorrow, but as time goes on, gratitude and celebration for his or her life often emerge. When a father stands with his daughter ready to give her away on her wedding day, there is celebration mixed with the sorrow of knowing the relationship will never be the same. At least on this side of eternity, deep sorrow and profound joy are often connected.

1. What is the most stressful time of moving that you have experienced?

_____

_____

_____

_____

_____

2. What makes moving so difficult?

_____

_____

_____

_____

_____

3. What are the challenges of moving from one stage to another (e.g., from college to young adult living, from having children at home to living as empty nesters, etc.)?

_____

_____

_____

_____

_____

4. What specific practices of corporate worship did the people reestablish when they returned to Jerusalem (see Ezra 3:2-6)? What was the significance of these spiritual practices?

_____

_____

_____

_____

_____

5. What practices of corporate worship are particularly meaningful to you and to your church family?

_____

_____

_____

_____

_____

6. What disciplines are a part of your regular spiritual practices? How do you assess and, when necessary, alter your personal and family spiritual rhythms?

_____

_____

_____

_____

_____

7. For the returning exiles, a big portion of doing God's work was finding their place in the temple construction project. What does "doing the work of the Lord" look like for you?

_____

_____

_____

_____

_____

8. What is the difference between doing the work of God and doing the work of the church? How do the work of God and the work of the church intersect?

_____

_____

_____

_____

_____

9. Share a time in your life when the words of Psalm 118:1 echoed in your soul: "Give thanks to the LORD for he is good; his love endures forever."

_____

_____

_____

_____

_____

10. Have you ever experienced a time when joy and sorrow intermingled to the point that they were indistinguishable? If you are willing, share your experience with your small group.

_____

_____

_____

_____

_____

Hitting the Wall

I am a runner. I did not mean to become a runner. I did not run growing up. I was never on a cross-country team and I have never won a distance race of any kind. I have never run a marathon, and to this point I have not broken the two-hour mark in the half marathon. I am only a runner because after I turned forty, I needed to lose weight, so along with some other fitness and lifestyle changes, I started running. It has helped me, but it is still one of the hardest things I do. When I run, birds do not sing, flowers do not open, and endorphins do not deliver a therapeutic rush of joy to my system. When I run, small animals get away because they are terrified of being crushed when I stumble in front of them. I am not graceful, athletic, or addicted to the feeling of running. I just run.

Sometimes, I run in races. I have had the privilege of running in the World's Best 10K in San Juan, Puerto Rico, twice with a friend who pastors in Carolina, Puerto Rico. If you are a runner and you can make it happen, this is a beautiful race. If you decide to run the World's Best 10K, however, you must accept two facts. First, the race is flat. Flat races are beautiful gifts to runners. Second, the race is hot. The average start temperature is 84 degrees in February. Most of us who live in the continental United States are not ready for running in 84 degrees in February, no matter how much we train. I know this from experience.

The first time I ran the World's Best 10K, I started in optimum running shape. I had hydrated appropriately for two weeks prior to the race. I was a well-oiled, reverend running machine. I had dreams of setting my personal record in a 10K. The first three miles of the event were perfection. My pace was excellent, my breathing optimal, and, though I was hot, I was not in any danger. I was in the training zone I had anticipated. Everything was working the way I expected. Then, mile 3.5 arrived, and I hit the wall. "Hitting the wall" is the runner phrase for when your energy completely disappears. Every step seems three times slower and more laborious than the step before. The air gets thick, your breathing is labored, and your muscles scream *"STOP!"* with every single fiber. This is hitting the wall. It is a lonely, painful place to be.

All runners know that "hitting the wall" is part of distance running. In each training run, in each race, you are going to reach the moment where your body says you cannot continue and you must will yourself forward. I was not surprised when I hit the wall in the World's Best 10K, but I was surprised by the intensity of the feeling. From mile 3.5 to mile 5, every muscle in my body wanted to quit the race. The heat sapped my strength more completely than I had anticipated. Somehow, I managed to keep putting one foot in front of the other. Just after mile 5, I began to see a clear path to the finish line 1 mile in the distance. Knowing the race was nearing its end gave me the adrenaline to pick up the pace and make it through. I did not reach my personal record, but I survived and outlasted the wall in hot running conditions. I was pleased.

Ezra 4 is the story of the returning exiles hitting the wall. They have dedicated and celebrated the foundation of the temple. As they prepare to begin the next phase of their building plan, however, they are confronted with a request from the peoples of the surrounding areas. These people offer to help with the construction efforts. Their reasoning is that they are worshipers of God as well, so they should have a hand in the construction of the temple.

These neighbors, however, have an agenda of their own. They are described as "enemies of Judah and Benjamin." These two names symbolize the returning exiles because before the exile, the southern kingdom of Judah was made up of the tribes of Judah and Benjamin. Why were the neighbors of the returning exiles enemies? As the text tells us, the neighboring peoples were not Jewish. Instead, they were conquered peoples who were settled in northern Jewish territories after Assyria defeated the kingdom of Israel in 722 BC. The Assyrian Empire practiced a ruthless policy of resettlement for all conquered peoples. When they conquered a nation, the people of that locale were removed to another place in the empire, and another conquered group was moved into the former land to take their place. This was a much different plan from the plan of King Cyrus that resettled conquered peoples, like the people of Judah, in their own homelands. So the neighbors of Judah were no longer the blood relatives of Israel. They were people from all over the globe who had been resettled to this particular area. In the resettlement process, people who moved into a new region would often add the faith practices of the region to their religious pantheon.

When the neighbors tell Zerubbabel and the heads of the families that they are also sacrificing to the God of Israel, then, they are speaking partial truth. They are sacrificing to Yahweh in addition to sacrificing to the other gods they follow. God's people are in a difficult position. Since they are a small group, it is tempting for them to accept all the help they can get. The problem, however, is that God gave them the first commandment as a part of their covenant responsibility: "you shall have no other gods before me." In other words, no other deity or priority can claim the devotion of the people of Israel. This was one of the great criticisms of kings of Israel and Judah before both were destroyed and taken captive. As the writer of 2 Kings explains about the exile of Israel and even the actions of Judah,

> They worshipped idols, though the LORD had said, "You shall not do this." The LORD warned Israel and Judah through all his prophets and seers, "Turn from your evil ways. Observe my commands and decrees, in accordance with the entire Law I commanded your fathers to obey and that I delivered to you through my servants and prophets." But they would not listen and were as stiff-necked as their fathers who did not trust in the LORD their God. (2 Kgs 17:12-14)

So Zerubbabel and the other leaders refuse to embrace the help of their neighbors because those neighbors are participating in the same divided worship of God that doomed their forefathers. Even though their refusal promises consequences, the leaders of the returned exiles are determined not to embrace a path way to syncretism (combining different belief systems).

In a pluralistic, international culture like the present-day United States of America, this exclusivist stance sounds harsh and outdated. My wife is a high school Spanish teacher. She once taught at a high school where her approximately 150 students represented at least 13 different countries of origin. She taught students whose families immigrated from Eritrea, Liberia, Iraq, Nepal, Vietnam, Mexico, and the Dominican Republic, just to name a few. Many of these students from around the world carry a Christian heritage and belief system. A number of them, however, represent religious backgrounds that two or three decades ago were rare in American life. Whether we like it or not, America is now home to Muslims, Hindus, Buddhists, and people who practice many other religions as well. Learning to share hospitality with those of different religious faiths who call our nation home is one of our profound growing edges as followers of Jesus. Sharing conversations, meals, and friendship with people of different (or no) faith traditions actually deepens our faith in Jesus and offers us the opportunity of loving like Jesus.

Immigration issues also connect to the lessons of Ezra 4. Our nation wrestles with how to treat immigrants and refugees in the face of fears regarding national security and biblical calls to love the "foreigner in our midst" (i.e., Exod 22:21, 23:9; Lev 19:33-34). The Paris attacks of November 2015 and the 2016 presidential election have pushed conversation about immigration and refugee care to a vitriolic level. The peoples living in the lands neighboring Jerusalem were afraid of the Jewish returnees. They responded to the exiles return with a false hospitality that sought control as opposed to welcome. How will we as a nation handle our own fears of immigrants and refugees? How will we balance our need for security with our call to extend God's love without manipulation or pretense?

There is another important question for us in the encounter between the people of Judah and their neighbors: How do minority religious groups embrace, renew, and share their religious identity? This question is prophetic on two levels. First, Christianity in American culture is now a minority movement. Christians used to enjoy a privileged status in American society. Now, we have to justify our voice and role at the table of community. Our voice used to matter because of our label. Now, we have to speak and, in many cases, overcome our label in order to be heard on an issue.

Sheer numbers are another fact depicting our move from the forefront to the minority edges of our culture. Studies tell us that American churches are in a dramatic decline that began in the 1960s. Only 18 percent of Americans are attending a church service on any given Sunday. The well-documented rise of the "spiritual but not religious" population continues to puzzle most churches. Together with these factors, the ever-decreasing number of adults in their twenties who attend church indicates the decrease of institutional Christian influence in American culture.[3] The question of how our churches, denominational groups, and Christian networks convert from the institutional Christianity that stood at the center of American culture to a grassroots Christianity that meets people in their neighborhoods is the defining transition for American churches of the current century. In any event, we must renew our commitment to following Jesus and participating in God's mission for the world from outside the lines of privilege. Like the returning exiles, we are a minority movement trusting God for direction and provision.

What a courageous stand the people of Judah took in the face of their neighbors! As a minority movement, they knew the risks. They knew they did not have the numbers to resist their enemies, but they knew they had a responsibility from God. They were called to rebuild the temple, restart temple worship, and fully recommit themselves to the ways of God. They committed themselves to this task without embracing the tantalizing dangers of syncretism.

Life in a minority movement is humbling. When you live as a part of the minority, you cannot win victories through frontal assaults or wielding greater power than others. You make progress through influence. In terms of our Christian witness in American culture, we make progress as a minority movement through love in our neighborhoods, prophetic truth-telling against injustice, prayers that seek renewal and transformation, and endurance in friendship and community development. The temptation for Christians in the United States is to adopt a sullen, nostalgic attitude where we lament that we are smaller than we once were, and then waste our resources trying to resurrect our institutional dominance. Instead, we can embrace our minority status, remembering that in Scripture, God works through the minority and people of insignificant status to accomplish God's mission.

The challenge, of course, is that God's people face opposition when in a minority role. The opposition the returning exiles faced only got worse when they refused the offer of help from their neighbors. In verses 4-5, the author of Ezra describes a pattern of active sabotage against the temple rebuilding efforts. This pattern of sabotage lasted for more than two decades until the temple was fully rebuilt and dedicated in 516 BC. For most of the two decades, the people did no work on the temple at all, as they wallowed in discouragement while their neighbors engaged the king of Persia to keep them from working. In the words of Ezra 4:24, "the work came to a standstill." As we mentioned at the beginning of this session, the opposition of their neighbors caused Judah to "hit the wall."

Before moving on, we need to note the interesting interpretive issues of Ezra 4:6-23. Mark A. Throntvelt, author of the *Ezra-Nehemiah* volume of the Interpretation commentary, has titled this section of the text "Back to the Future." This section reminds us of the chronological redirections that make Ezra-Nehemiah so difficult to read. The letters included in this section of Scripture were written many years after the work on the temple addressed in Ezra 4:1-5 and 24.[4] King Xerxes I reigned from 486–465 BC while Artaxerxes I reigned from 465–424 BC. We are reminded, therefore, that the work of Ezra-Nehemiah is a compilation of primary sources and editorial writings designed for telling the story of God's activity in restoring the people of Judah after the exile. The primary purpose of Ezra-Nehemiah is not to give a chronological rendering of the history of the restoration period; instead, the compiler shares the story of the people's calling from God, the ongoing opposition the people faced in living out their calling from God, and the faithfulness of God in continuing to deliver the people in the midst of opposition.

The letters to King Xerxes and King Artaxerxes illustrate that over the years, the descendants of the returned exiles face the same opposition and persecution that affected their ancestors upon their initial return from exile. The story has not changed. Even though the new temple has been completed for decades by the time of the letters to Xerxes and Artaxerxes, the minority remnant of Judah continues to face opposition from all sides. The opposition uses duplicitous tactics, telling Artaxerxes that once the city of Jerusalem is rebuilt, no new taxes or tribute will be paid by the people of Judah (vv. 13-14), and the opponents of Judah go so far as to label Jerusalem a historically "rebellious and seditious" city. The compiler of Ezra-Nehemiah includes these out-of-chronological-order letters to emphasize one point to his contemporary readers: they are facing the same oppression and calling to endure what their parents and grandparents faced decades ago.

In truth, followers of Jesus today still face the same misunderstanding, misrepresentation, and oppression that the remnant of Judah faced in the days of the restoration. We face misunderstanding when people decide that all followers of Jesus are identical to the portrayals of Christians in the mainstream media. We face misrepresentation when other Christians and non-Christians claim to speak what we believe, and then spew a message far different from the call of love and justice that God in Christ Jesus entrusted to us.

We face some forms of oppression whenever neighbors treat us with suspicion or polite reservation when they find out we are followers of Jesus. Of course, around the world, we know that brothers and sisters in Christ are facing the oppression of injustice, prison, and even genocide as a result of their faith. For all of the tolerance pronounced in our era, we still face oppression, and in fact, we are often guilty of showering oppressive ridicule and disdain on others when they disagree with us.

In truth, discouragement is our greatest threat. How easy it was for the returning exiles to cower in discouragement due to their neighbors' continued opposition and disruption. How easy it is for us to succumb to discouragement when we wait for God to act in the life of a hurting loved one, and over the weeks and months we see no evidence of change. How easy it is for us to look across the faces of our churches, the spiritual practices of our communities, and the brokenness of injustice in our cities and wonder if God's work is actually making progress. Even in moments of decline and desperation, we must remember that discouraging words and thoughts are not from God.

1. Have you ever experienced a "hit the wall" moment in something you were trying to do? What did it feel like? How did you continue forward until you finished?

_____

_____

_____

_____

_____

2. Think of and list ways that offers of help from people can be more self-serving than sincere. (For example, a payday lender offers to help you make ends meet by giving you the funds from your paycheck a couple of days early.)

_____

_____

_____

_____

_____

3. Have you ever had a friend, coworker, or family member extend a manipulative offer of help to you? How did it feel? What was your response?

_____

_____

_____

_____

_____

4. When was the last time you had a conversation about religion with a friend or neighbor who was not a Christian? What did you learn?

_____

_____

_____

_____

_____

5. What would be the most difficult part about resettling to a new country, particularly if it happened quickly? How can you or your class be a neighbor in the name of Jesus to people recently relocated to the United States?

_____

_____

_____

_____

_____

6. What is the greatest opposition you face in living as a follower of Jesus?

_____

_____

_____

_____

_____

7. What opposition does your church or small group face in living out its calling to follow Jesus in your culture?

_____

_____

_____

_____

_____

8. If you are willing to share, tell a story about the greatest opposition you have ever faced as a follower of Jesus. How did you handle this opposition?

_____

_____

_____

_____

_____

9. In what ways are you discouraged in your life today? How do you handle discouragement?

_____

_____

_____

_____

_____

10. Whom is God calling you to encourage today? What specific action(s) can your class or group do to encourage others in your congregation and in your community?

_____

_____

_____

_____

_____

From Inertia to Engagement

Text: Ezra 5:1-5; 6:1-5, 13-22
Background text: Haggai 1

I am not in my customary, comfortable writing space as I begin this session. Rather than relaxing in a restaurant or coffee shop with a large glass of sweet tea, I am in an aisle seat on an airplane waiting for clearance to take off. Of course, I am supposed to have my laptop turned off and stowed away at this time, but moments ago, the course of my journey was altered. The captain's voice came over the intercom and said, "Ladies and gentlemen, due to the heavy weather in front of us, our flight is going to be delayed for an hour and forty minutes. We are trying to see if we can return to a gate."

Since I am in Atlanta, I had an idea of what was coming next.

"Ladies and gentlemen, there are no empty gates that can accept us at this time, so we are going to have to wait here on the taxi way. Hopefully, the tower will accelerate our departure due to our conditions."

As of this moment, our conditions have not accelerated, so I decided to write.

Unexpected—and often depressed—waiting is a major theme of the Ezra-Nehemiah story. At the end of Ezra 4, the writer describes the he people of Judah's wait to finish the temple. For two decades, they were cowered by the tactics of the neighboring peoples. During this time, a deep spiritual and physical lethargy developed. It is not hard to imagine the returning exiles struggling to produce a living in the midst of opposition with limited resources. Their waiting degenerated into a sullen, apathetic day-to-day existence with little, if any, vision for the restoration God had planned for Jerusalem.

This malaise went on for twenty years until the prophets Haggai and Zechariah began preaching to the people. Ezra 5:1-2 gives a brief overview of the work of these prophets and the restart of the work by Zerubbabel and Joshua. The report in verses 1-2 is profoundly understated. Moving a people from inertia to engagement is a Herculean task, particularly when the inertia develops due to fear and opposition. Haggai and Zechariah, however, received a word from the Lord, and they proclaimed with power and passion that the day of apathy was past, and the time for zeal had arrived.

> Thus says the LORD of hosts: Consider how you have fared. Go up to the hills and bring wood and build the house, so that I may take pleasure in it and be honored, says the LORD. You have looked for much, and, lo, it came to little; and when you brought it home, I blew it away. Why? says the LORD of hosts. Because my house lies in ruins, while all of you hurry off to your own houses. (Hag 1:7-9 NRSV)

In all fairness, the people of Judah had shown some zeal and initiative during the twenty-year lapse in temple work, but they focused their energy on building their own homes! God's house, and the worship of God, became afterthoughts. So Haggai told the people to "consider how you have fared." He wanted them to ponder if there was a connection between their anemic harvests and their half-hearted devotion to God. In fact, God spelled out the connection for the people, telling them through Haggai that when the people ignored God's house of worship, even though God provided their deliverance from the land of Babylon, God ignored their attempts to establish a sense of roots and prosperity.

The people experienced poverty as a result of their disobedience to God's direction. The theological understanding of the Old Testament, known as Deuteronomic Theology, holds that the covenant relationship between the people of Israel and God functions according to obedience and blessing. If the people obey the covenant commands of God, they live within the blessing of God. If the people live in disobedience, including allowing other priorities to determine their direction and purpose, then they live outside the blessing of God.

The values presented in Deuteronomic Theology are troubling to us. While the so-called American dream echoes similar sentiments, people have discovered that the ones who do right do not always prosper, and the ones who engage in unjust business practices often reap rewards. There is a fundamental lack of fairness and justice regarding material and many times relational prosperity.

Books in the Old Testament, including Job and Ecclesiastes, wrestle with the questions of just persons enduring hardship and unjust persons experiencing blessing. When he confronts the blind man in John 9, Jesus tells his disciples that the man is not blind because of his sin, but his blindness provides an opportunity for God to work. Other passages of Scripture, along with our own life experiences, teach us that obedience to God is not a guarantee of material or relational blessing.

And yet disobedience to God is a guarantee of brokenness. When the returning exiles disconnected from God, they embraced a season of spiritual apathy. In the hard days of opposition to the temple rebuilding, the people did not turn and find strength in the Lord. Instead, they built their homes and attempted to cultivate their own comfort and security. The whole-hearted pursuit of comfort and security with only nominal connection to God is its own form of brokenness. It is a brokenness that separates one from the peace, compassion, grace, and love found in full relationship with God. Sin may not guarantee material poverty on a personal level, but it definitively separates people from the blessing of deep and vibrant life with God.

But God's word breaks through our brokenness. In the case of the exiles who laid the foundation of the temple only to have their efforts stymied by opposition and malaise, God spoke through the prophetic voices of Haggai and Zechariah, and the people recommitted themselves to the temple work. The words of Haggai are powerful as he describes the people returning to the work:

> And the LORD stirred up the spirit of Zerubbabel son of Shealtiel, governor of Judah, and the spirit of Joshua son of Jehozadak, the high priest, and the spirit of all the remnant of the people; and they came and worked on the house of the LORD of hosts, their God, on the twenty-fourth day of the month, in the sixth month. (Hag 1:14-15)

What a powerful word! The LORD stirred up the spirit of Zerubbabel, Joshua, and the whole group of the returned exiles. People who passed by the temple site for years without lifting a stone were filled with reverence for the LORD and the desire to finish the temple. They repented of their apathy and self-absorption and embraced the prophetic imagination of Haggai and Zechariah. Even when Tattenai and the leaders of the other people groups in the area challenged them, the remnant of Judah refused to back down. Under the prophetic leadership of Haggai and Zechariah, a people who were once powerless in doing God's work emerged as a determined, coordinated community of faith committed to doing God's mission. The change in attitude, motivation, and passion represented a paradigmatic shift in direction for God's people.

What does it take for people in our present culture to hear God's call to embrace God's coming in the world? God's people are called to work with God in inaugurating the rule of God on earth, in every area of life, and yet, far too often, we fall short of this call. A couple of years ago, I attended the inaugural Mission lectures at the McAfee School of Theology at Mercer University. Alan Roxburgh was the lecturer, and his first lecture focused on the depths of decline in the churches of North America. He noted, like many others, that churches in North America have entered a new era, a time where efforts to promote the institutional health of our churches and denominations are growing more fruitless. We work diligently, doing the same things that used to work, but to no avail. Then, we change the packaging of our attempts to grow and make the church accessible to people who are disinterested in the church, but these efforts fall flat as well. This has led the churches of North America into a new reality of institutional peril punctuated by an ever-deepening malaise. People in North America are spiritually interested but completely disinterested in church, and this truth has sent North American Christianity into a tailspin.

The future for North American churches, like the future of the temple building project and the full restoration of the remnant of the people of Judah, appears bleak. And yet Roxburgh dared to suggest a prophetic and remarkable notion: What if the chaos we are experiencing is not the destruction of North American Christianity as we know it? What if, instead, God's Spirit is blowing through the malaise of our institutions to call us back to the real work of God's mission? What if the decline and disintegration of our institutions is really God at work making all things new? To put it in terms of Haggai, what if we are living in a time where God is stirring up our spirits and calling us not to the maintenance of a secure church, family, and work life but instead to the adventure of embodying God's love in our neighborhoods? What if the brokenness and chaos is where God is doing God's work? Maybe, like the remnant from the exile, we are called to embrace God's work in the midst of chaos and to move forward in obedience, regardless of our fear.

Fear. At one time, years before, the people of Judah succumbed to it. Now, when the opposition threatens them, they keep working and craft their own case for King Darius of Persia, the king who followed Cyrus. While the letter of decision is on its way to Darius, the people continue working because God has given them strength and favor so that they will not give up. They refuse to be bullied by the neighbors around them, even though as a people, they are smaller. A people who cowered in fear for nearly twenty years is learning how to live in the strength of the LORD.

Eventually, King Darius returns his decision to the people of Judah. Unlike the later letters we read in Ezra 4 to King Xerxes and Artaxerxes, Darius gives the people of Judah a rousing endorsement. He not only affirms that Cyrus gave the command to the Jews to rebuild the temple but also reaffirms that the rebuilding cost is the responsibility of the royal treasury. Furthermore, Darius tells Tattenai and the other leaders in the Trans-Euphrates region that the temple rebuilding project is a Jewish responsibility. Those leaders are to keep away from the site and cease all interference in Jewish affairs. The timing of the preaching of Haggai and Zechariah was God's timing. Now the people are ready to embrace the work, and King Darius affirms the work. Like King Cyrus before him, Darius is used to do the work of God's redemption.

There is nothing like a dose of much-needed encouragement to push people into higher levels of effort. The people of Israel were already working hard, spurred on by the Spirit of God and the prophetic words of Haggai and Zechariah. The endorsement from King Darius, however, added wind to the sails of their efforts. The people worked with all their might until at last, the work on the temple was completed in 516 BC.

Ezra 5:16 tells us that the people of Israel celebrated the dedication of the house of God with joy. This seems like a gross understatement by the author. After all, a sacrifice of 100 bulls, 200 hundred rams, 400 male lambs, and the symbolic 12 male goats represents more than the typical excitement of a spiritual tailgate. Instead, the worship of the people on this occasion wells up from the depths of their being. The emotion of their disappointments, setbacks, and fears gives way to the ecstasy of seeing the fruit of obedience and perseverance. Haggai called the people to move forward in rebuilding the temple according to God's commands, and God faithfully honored their work by protecting them from their neighbors and giving them favor with King Darius.

From Inertia to Engagement

To see this celebration as merely the final celebration commemorating a critical accomplishment, however, would be shortsighted. The reason for the celebration is not only the completion of the temple. The primary reason for it is the recognition that the power and intervention of God have made the completion of the temple possible. God called the people to do the work, and in their earliest years of return from exile, they grew discouraged due to the opposition of their neighbors. When God stirred up the spirit of Zerubbabel through the prophets Haggai and Zechariah, however, the people engaged the work of building the temple with renewed commitment. God honored their obedience with protection. The people obeyed God's direction through the words of the prophets, and through their obedience, they experienced God's blessing. The people, therefore, are now celebrating God's faithfulness to them along with celebrating their own renewal of covenant relationship with God. We see evidence of the reaffirmation of their covenant relationship as they celebrate the festival of Passover. In practicing Passover, the returned exiles reassert their connection to celebrating the deliverance God provided for their ancestors in Egypt and to them as they returned from Babylon. They also relearn the lesson of covenant obedience; following God's direction leads to blessing and divine protection, while following one's own agenda often leads to negative consequences.

We can learn two important lessons from the worship celebration of the people of Israel that will enhance our corporate worship. First, corporate worship must strive to connect all generations to the faithfulness of God in the past, present, and future. Too often, worship services are unintentionally only for adults, while children and teenagers miss vital teaching moments to hear the faith of past generations explained in a way they can understand. Furthermore, we struggle to connect our worship services to the ancient practices of faith that encourage people to participate in worship rather than serving as mere spectators. Worship planners must take seriously the challenge of introducing symbols, rituals, and ancient practices of faith into corporate worship without insulating themselves from innovations that draw worshipers deeper into conversation with God.

Second, the people of Israel worshiped with an overwhelming sense of joy and expectation. Their joy emerged from gratitude for what God had done, and their sense of expectation came from the belief that God was not finished! Too often, worship services in

American culture are filled with either an overabundance of ecstatic emotionalism or a repetitive pattern of formality that, if changed, leaves worshipers disappointed and confused. The joyful expectation and, indeed, the full story of the people of Israel following the prophetic words of Haggai remind us that worshiping God is anything but sanitary and predictable. Instead, worship is where God calls us to challenges beyond our strength and where we celebrate with grateful joy the Spirit of God that empowers us to rise up and accomplish tasks that are only possible with God. Too often we settle for corporate worship that is static and predictable, whereas God is dynamic and untamed.

Finally, the story of the people of Israel recommitting to rebuilding the temple of God offers insight into how God partners with people to do God's work in the world. We are tempted to pray and ask God for deliverance from our troubles, or to plead with God for justice to emerge in our world. The truth is, God most often answers these prayers not with a sweeping wave of God's hand but through "stirring up the spirits of individuals" to own their plights and take initiative in moving forward with God toward deliverance. In the case of seeking justice for the world, God's Spirit will convict a person of the need for deeper justice or advocacy in a particular arena, and this individual, inspired and empowered by the Spirit of God, will take the initiative to work for justice. God chooses to work through people to establish God's kingdom in the world. We are blessed to live as participants in God's salvific action, to join our gifts with God's greatness for the sake of the kingdom of God.

1. Describe a time when you were forced to wait longer than you expected. How did you pass the time? What did you do to maintain your self-control?

_____

_____

_____

_____

2. What is the hardest wait you have endured in your life?

_____

_____

_____

_____

_____

3. Why did the people of Israel wait for twenty years to resume the work of rebuilding the temple of God?

_____

_____

_____

_____

_____

4. How would you have responded to the chastising words of Haggai? Whom do you allow to tell you hard truths?

_____

_____

_____

_____

_____

5. What do you think of the idea of Deuteronomic Theology mentioned above and exemplified in Haggai 1:5-11? How does this theological framework make sense? How does Deuteronomic Theology fall short in speaking about how God works?

_____

_____

_____

_____

_____

6. How do the people of Israel handle the opposition of their neighbors once they return to the temple work?

_____
_____
_____
_____
_____

7. Have you ever felt the Lord "stirring up" your spirit? What task was God calling you to undertake?

_____
_____
_____
_____
_____

8. How does God "stir up" the spirit of a congregation? When has God "stirred up" the spirit of your church?

_____
_____
_____
_____
_____

9. How does the corporate worship of your church involve all generations? How are children taught to worship in your congregation?

_____
_____
_____
_____
_____

10. How is joy present in your personal worship of God? How is joy present in the corporate worship of your congregation?

_____

_____

_____

_____

_____

11. Where is God most actively at work in your life? In your church? In your neighborhood?

_____

_____

_____

_____

_____

The Return of the Law

Central Text: Ezra 7:6-10, 13-17, 25-26
Background Text: Ezra 7

As a pastor, I have attended and officiated a number of weddings. Celebrating the love and commitment of a husband and wife in worship is one of the highlights of my calling. The conversations leading up to the wedding, the anticipation present in the voices and faces of the future bride and groom, and the wedding service itself are nearly always filled with joy and hope. They are treasures of celebration.

Wedding receptions, however, are sometimes difficult for me. Perhaps they are for you as well. You see, after the momentous presentation, "My friends, I now present to you Mr. and Mrs. So and So," the congregation is primed to celebrate. We move to the reception location and then, most of the time, we wait. We are bursting to share celebration with the happy couple, but they are nowhere to be found. So we wait. We eat hors d'oeuvres and share conversation with one another, but it is all a matrimonial filibuster, the preamble to the real celebration. After all, if the bride and groom are missing, the party is not complete.

Does it seem strange that we have moved through six chapters of the book of Ezra, and we have not even met Ezra yet? The events of Ezra 6 conclude in 516 BC. Ezra 7, which tells the story of Ezra the priest's commission to return to Jerusalem, takes place around the year 458 BC! There are sixty years between the final foundational stories of the return of the exiles to Jerusalem and the arrival of Ezra in Jerusalem. All of the important lessons we have learned to this point were gleaned from the preamble to the story. Now, in Ezra 7, we arrive at the main character and at the theme that underlies the story of the book of Ezra. Now that all the characters have come to the reception hall, let's begin the new story!

What do we know about Ezra? First, the compiler of Ezra makes clear Ezra's connection to the priestly line of Israel. According to the genealogy of the author in Ezra 7:1-6, Ezra is directly descended from the line of Aaron, the chief priest. The writer is not as concerned with genealogical fact as he is with establishing Ezra's priestly authority. Ezra is given the charge by King Artaxerxes to assess the condition of Jewish religious practice in Jerusalem and to make amends to the practices according to his knowledge and understanding of God's laws. One cannot have the mandate to reform the temple and faith practices of the people without priestly authority. Therefore, the author clarifies the priestly credentials of Ezra at the outset.

Ezra, however, is more than a priest: "he was a teacher well-versed in the Law of Moses." Ezra is not a priest merely due to title or lineage; rather, he is a priest who has a deep love for the law of God. Ezra 7:10 tells us that Ezra devoted himself to the study and observance of the law. He was not only a student of the law of God but was also a faithful follower of the Law. So Ezra was a spiritual sage who influenced a spiritual renewal of the people and also carried a deep connection to God and the practices of living under God's direction. Ezra was a teacher and spiritual leader of the people in every sense.

Second, Ezra served as an official representative from the court of King Artaxerxes of Persia. Since Ezra was charged with going to Jerusalem as his representative, it is likely that he served in connection with the court, perhaps advising the king and his ministers on matters related to Jewish law, culture, and religion. It is obvious that Artaxerxes held Ezra in high esteem since he gave him such wide-ranging powers and responsibilities for his assignment in Jerusalem. Among other duties, Ezra was charged with investigating the state of the law and practices of temple worship in Jerusalem, refitting the temple with precious articles and worship accessories, purchasing sacrifices and other items needed for worship, selecting judges and magistrates for the people, and making sure the people were trained in the knowledge and practice of the law of the Lord. Ezra, as a representative of the king, was entrusted with great power, opportunity, and responsibility.

Finally, Ezra saw his assignment from Artaxerxes as the continuing salvific action of God on behalf of the Jewish people. Notice Ezra 7:27-28:

Blessed be the LORD, the God of our ancestors, who put such a thing as this into the heart of the king to glorify the house of the LORD in Jerusalem, and who extended to me steadfast love before the king and his counselors, and before all the king's mighty officers. I took courage, for the hand of the LORD my God was upon me, and I gathered leaders from Israel to go up with me. (NRSV)

The book of Ezra begins with the author claiming God's providential work in the actions and commands of King Cyrus to return the people of Israel to Jerusalem. King Darius, likewise, gives official permission for the people to continue the work on the temple inspired by the work of Haggai and Zechariah. Now, King Artaxerxes gives Ezra the mission to return to Jerusalem to assess the religious condition of the people and to train them in the law of the Lord. Later, we will see King Artaxerxes respond favorably to Nehemiah's request to return to Jerusalem to rebuild the city wall and govern the people. Clearly, the writer of Ezra wants the people of Israel to understand a vital faith lesson: even though Jerusalem is still subject to the ruler of the Persian Empire, the king is subject to the commands and direction of God. God is more powerful than empires and nations. In fact, the wisdom of God can even use the apparatus of empire to accomplish the purpose and justice of God.

Before moving on with Ezra's return to Jerusalem, we must address an important question Ezra's character raises. What place does the law of God have in our lives? Put another way, how does Scripture impact our lives on a daily basis? Ezra was known even by Artaxerxes as "one who possessed the wisdom of God" (see Ezra 7:25). He possessed the wisdom of God because he was a student of the Pentateuch, the first five books of the Old Testament. He had learned them well and they shaped his character, decision-making, and leadership.

In a culture where biblical literacy has rapidly declined, it is more necessary than ever for followers of Jesus to ingest and digest the words of Scripture. There are many misconceptions regarding the belief structure and practices of Christianity. How will we discuss questions from curious inquirers if we have not studied the Bible and prepared ourselves in prayer for compassionate conversations? How will biblically informed decisions involving difficult ethical and justice questions happen if followers of Jesus are not immersed in the wisdom of the Scriptures? How will thoughtful Christians counter misrepresentations and misinterpretations of Scripture if they are not grounded in the Scriptures themselves? Furthermore, Jesus followers must invest in Scripture study in order to clearly retell our story in a culture that does not know the basic facts of the Christian message. In fact, according to a 2015 survey from the Pew Research Center, nearly 23 percent of adult Americans identify as "nones," meaning they identify as atheist, agnostic, or "nothing in particular." In addition, studies have suggested that only 18 percent of Americans are in a worship service on a regular Sunday. So, in a culture where active Christian discipleship is a minority movement, followers of Jesus must know and appropriately tell the scriptural story of their faith.

We must address one more point regarding the study of Scripture: the study of Scripture must not only create persons who are repositories of biblical knowledge. It must also transform individuals into more just, loving, compassionate, and forgiving Christ-followers. Reading Scripture must lead us to diligently embrace and depict the love and grace of Jesus. Meditating on Scripture must lead us to a life of deeper devotion to Jesus and away from the siren calls of sin that permeate the air of our culture and saturate the fields of our minds. We mediate on the word of God to protect and prepare ourselves for spiritual transformation. The writers of Scripture knew the power of meditating on the wisdom of God's law for spiritual transformation. Consider these texts:

> I treasure your word in my heart, so that I may not sin against you.
> Blessed are you, O LORD; teach me your statutes.
> With my lips I declare all the ordinances of your mouth.
> I delight in the way of your decrees as much as in all riches.
> I will meditate on your precepts, and fix my eyes on your ways.
> I will delight in your statutes; I will not forget your word.
> (Ps 119:11-16)

> Let the word of Christ dwell in you richly; teach and admonish one another in all wisdom; and with gratitude in your hearts sing psalms, hymns, and spiritual songs to God. (Col 3:16)

Ezra did not merely know the word of God; instead, he was transformed by the word of God. If we are to grow deeply in our relationship with God, we must read God's word until it "dwells in us richly," until it is "treasured in our heart." We must make space in our lives with God's word so that the Holy Spirit can use the word of God to change us:

> Often we are so burdened and overwhelmed with other thoughts, images, and concerns that it may take a long time before God's Word has swept all else aside and come through. . . . This is the very reason why we begin our meditation with prayer that God may send His Holy Spirit to us through His Word and reveal His Word to us and enlighten us.[5]

Ezra organizes his return to Jerusalem along with the group of men listed in Ezra 8:1-14, along with women, children, and servants. The group meets by the Ahava Canal in Babylon to prepare for their journey. They handle tasks of organization, but, more important, they proclaim a fast. With this fast, the people ask for God's protection and humble themselves before God's goodness. Ezra looks to God for security, even refusing to ask the king for soldiers to protect them on their journey.

Ezra also begins carrying out the tasks assigned by the king even before they arrive in Jerusalem. In 8:24-27, Ezra chooses twenty-four leading priest and entrusts them with a critical task. They will have the responsibility of inventorying, carrying, and protecting the gold, silver, and bronze articles set aside for the temple of God. These items are weighed and cataloged before the journey. Once they arrive in Jerusalem, the twenty-four priests will take the items to the temple. There, they will weigh them and make certain that all items consecrated to God are deposited in the temple.

This is a weighty responsibility. Carrying, preserving, and protecting the consecrated articles of God are sacred actions. The people of Israel have experienced much suffering during the exile as a result of treating what is sacred with contempt, and treating what is profane as precious. Ezra must choose wisely. If the twenty-four he chooses love the allure of gold more than their devotion to God, they will take the items for themselves rather than preserve them for the house of God. The Old Testament is filled with stories of Israelites taking what does not belong to them in disobedience to God's direction (see for example Achan, Josh 7:1, 10-13; Elisha's servant, Gehazi, 2 Kgs 5:15-16, 19-27; and Manasseh, 1 Kgs 21:9). In the case of Manasseh, he built altars in the temple of the LORD that honored himself. Idolatry, in all its forms, was a primary sin of Judah that led to exile. Now, Ezra must choose priests of noble character who will not fall prey to the lust for gold and recognition. How would these priests, who have only had training in the law from Ezra, handle their sacred calling when their ancestors failed so miserably?

Ezra and his caravan arrived in Jerusalem in 458 BC, kept safe from the trials of their journey by the hand of God. After three days' rest, the caravan goes to the temple where the twenty-four priests deposit their gold, silver, and bronze. Ezra 8:33-34 tells the result: "Everything was accounted for by number and weight, and the entire weight was recorded at that time" (NIV). The priests acted with integrity. They brought every last consecrated article to the temple. Where many of their ancestors had failed, these priests upheld the trust Ezra placed in them, and they began a new time of spiritual renewal with an action of devotion. The priests and the returned exiles then sacrificed to the LORD, including a sin offering on behalf of all the people. Ezra's arrival to assess the religious practice of the people is now complete.

Ezra's decision regarding the twenty-four priests offers an important example for anyone contemplating significant people decisions. On a regular basis, we all have to make decisions about whom we will trust with significant responsibilities. Which friends will you really talk through your struggles with, and which friends will you relegate to surface-level conversations? Whom will you trust to baby-sit your children? Which contracting company will you choose to renovate your kitchen? Which direct report will you trust to handle a significant project that reflects on you? What counselor will you trust when your marriage is struggling? In all of these and so many other critical decisions, we confront the basic question: how do we make good decisions about the people we trust in our lives?

Ezra does not give us a set of step-by-step instructions on how to choose trustworthy people. In fact, as much as we may want it to be, the Bible is not merely a step-by-step instruction book for living. Instead, the Bible is the story of how God works through people to bring redemption to all creation. In the pieces of God's story in Scripture, we encounter the movement of God's Holy Spirit in our lives. So Ezra's story of thoughtfully choosing these twenty-four priests resonates with the times we have sought wisdom from God regarding the critical and difficult decisions of our lives. Certainly, we do not see the logistics of Ezra's decision-making, but we can imagine the conversations, soul-searching, and prayers that went into his discernment process. So perhaps the best question for anyone looking to improve his personal decision-making is how to grow one's skills in discernment.

Again, we do not have a paragraph in Ezra's story that tells us how to get better at discernment, but we know that Ezra was known for his deep connection to the word and wisdom of God. When we face difficult decisions, we need more than knowledge and information. We need the wisdom to process knowledge, information, and understanding and synthesize them into wise decisions and motivations for living. Ezra made wise decisions because he immersed himself in the law of God, and in God's law, he found wisdom for discerning his life direction. Immersing oneself in the wisdom of God leads to wise decision-making. This is the underlying theme of the book of Proverbs. The author writes as a father giving counsel to his son:

> Get wisdom, get understanding; do not forget my words or turn away from them. Do not forsake wisdom, and she will protect you; love her, and she will watch over you. The beginning of wisdom is this: Get wisdom. Though it cost all you have, get understanding. (Prov 4:5-7 NIV)

Wisdom and discernment are essential to good decision-making and effective leadership. In the remaining sessions of our study, we will see the importance of wise discernment in the leadership of Ezra and Nehemiah.

1. What is the most interesting story you remember from a wedding reception? What is the longest you ever waited for the bride and groom to arrive at a wedding reception?

_____

_____

_____

_____

_____

The Return of the Law

2. Why does it take the writer of Ezra so long to introduce Ezra into the story?

_____

_____

_____

_____

_____

3. What do you imagine was happening during the sixty-year interlude between the end of Ezra 6 and the beginning of Ezra 7? What do you think life was like during this time for the people in Jerusalem?

_____

_____

_____

_____

_____

4. How does Artaxerxes' mission for Ezra in Ezra 7 remind you of the commands of Cyrus to the original returning exiles in Ezra 1?

_____

_____

_____

_____

_____

5. How do you rationalize the response of King Artaxerxes in Ezra 4:18-24 with the charge given to Ezra in 7:11-28? How can Artaxerxes support the opposition in the first text and then send Ezra on a mission of encouragement to the people of Jerusalem in the second?

_____

_____

_____

_____

_____

6. Ezra is described as one who "devoted himself to the study and observance of the Law of the LORD . . ." (Ezra 7:10). Using this information and your imagination, describe what you think Ezra was like.

_____
_____
_____
_____
_____

7. How would you describe the difference between having knowledge about the Bible and knowing the Bible?

_____
_____
_____
_____
_____

8. What regular practices do you embrace in order to devote yourself to the word of God? Which practices are most helpful to you?

_____
_____
_____
_____
_____

9. What are your struggles when it comes to reading and meditating on Scripture? How can your class or small group encourage one another in these struggles?

_____
_____
_____
_____
_____

10. When you face hard decisions, what are the key parts of your decision-making process?

_____

_____

_____

_____

_____

11. Describe a time where God's wisdom helped you make a difficult decision.

_____

_____

_____

_____

_____

12. If you are willing, describe a time when you made a poor decision. What role did God's wisdom play in that decision? What would you do differently if you were making the decision over again?

_____

_____

_____

_____

_____

An Unrelenting Burden

Text: Nehemiah 1

After spending our first five study sessions in the book of Ezra, it is time to direct our attention to the book of Nehemiah. As mentioned in the introduction above, Ezra and Nehemiah were actually considered one book in early Jewish tradition. The two books interweave themes, stories, and characters in such a fashion that the chronology of the story and the relationship between the persons of Ezra and Nehemiah are difficult to untangle. In fact, scholars have wrestled for years with whether Ezra arrived before Nehemiah in Jerusalem (traditional view), or if Ezra actually arrived after Nehemiah (various other views). The question of who arrived first is far from settled in the minds of many scholars, and good points are raised from many directions related to the information in the text. This conversation, while interesting, is beyond the purview of our discussion. As stated in the introduction above, for the ease of interpretation and application, this volume follows the traditional interpretation that Ezra arrived in Jerusalem before Nehemiah (458 BC) and Nehemiah arrived approximately thirteen years later (445 BC). While there is much debate regarding Ezra's date of arrival, there is general agreement among scholars on the time of Nehemiah's return to Jerusalem.

What do we know about Nehemiah? First, we know he is the cupbearer to King Artaxerxes (Neh 11:1b). The responsibility of the cupbearer was to provide the king with wine for his meals or at any other occasion it was requested. By bringing wine to the king, the cupbearer certified that the wine was safe for the king to drink. The position of cupbearer was significant in the court of the king of Persia. Intrigue was part of the fabric of the royal house, especially since Artaxerxes' father Xerxes was killed by his own servant in his bedchamber. Servant positions that guarded the life of the king carried considerable prestige and required the highest level of trust. It speaks well of Nehemiah that he, a foreigner, is trusted completely by King Artaxerxes. Nehemiah's position of responsibility gives him special access and favor from the king.

Second, we know Nehemiah is an Israelite. In Nehemiah 1:2, Nehemiah seeks out information regarding the status of the city of Jerusalem and the exiles who have returned. He is looking for news from one of his brothers, Hanani, who has recently returned from Jerusalem with a group of other men. Though Nehemiah has crafted an exceptional life for himself in Persia and, indeed, has likely lived all of his life in Persia, he remembers and values his roots. He is Jewish and he longs for the prosperity of his people.

Third, unlike Ezra, Nehemiah is not a priest. Nehemiah's relationship to God is vitally important to him and to the story of the book of Nehemiah, but he is never noted as anything more than what we would call a layperson. His faith matters to him, but he is not a member of any professional religious group. Instead, he is a civic leader whose faith informs how he leads and governs.

The purpose of Nehemiah 1 is to introduce the reader to Nehemiah and, more important, to acquaint the reader with Nehemiah's passion. The reader does not have to wait long to discover the burden that despairs and drives Nehemiah. When he asks his brother, Hanani, for a report from Jerusalem, he is given disappointing news. The people in Jerusalem are "in great trouble and disgrace" (v. 3). Furthermore, the walls of the city are burned and broken down. One will remember that the walls of the city of Jerusalem were destroyed by Nebuchadnezzar in 587 BC as part of the destruction of Jerusalem. Since that time, the returning exiles had rebuilt the temple foundation (536 BC) and completed the rebuilding of the temple (516 BC), crafted homes for their families and sowed fields for food, and figured out ways to scratch out an existence in a dangerous and constantly changing setting where they faced opposition at every turn. It was a precarious existence, even with Ezra's arrival nearly fourteen years prior.

The state of the Jewish returnees dismays Nehemiah. He mourns and weeps bitterly over the condition of Jerusalem and its people. It is the burden that will not let him go, though he mourns, weeps, and prays; the burden of the remnant in Jerusalem, unprotected behind a burned and broken wall, is seared into his soul. This is not the weeping of a man who sees a documentary and is moved to write a blog post. This is not the mourning of one who weeps for a day until he feels better. This is not the sadness of a person who feels a deep sense of compassion for a people she encounters on a mission trip only to find that, over time, the sense of connection fades. Nehemiah's burden for the plight of the people in Jerusalem is in front of his mind day and night. It will not let him go.

Can you think of a time when you were overwhelmed by the needs of a group of people or angered by an injustice in the world? Do you know what it feels like to be so consumed with passion for a need in your community, church, or world that it overwhelms the full layers of your thoughts and emotions? In the Baptist network known as the Cooperative Baptist Fellowship (CBF), members challenge one another to embrace the burdens of others and advocate on their behalf. Stephen Reeves, Associate Coordinator for Advocacy and Partnership, describes advocacy as

> . . . to speak out on behalf of another, to take their concerns as your own and use your voice to help change that problem or situation. While this can certainly be accomplished by seeking a change in public policy at the local, state or federal level, it can also be done on an individual basis through non-policy means.[6]

The point is that followers of Jesus are called to speak out on behalf of others, particularly those who are experiencing economic, social, and personal injustice. The brokenness of others must lead us to mourn, like the brokenness of the people in Jerusalem led Nehemiah to weep.

We must, however, do more than weep. The pain of the Jerusalem exiles led Nehemiah to take on the plight of his people. Their plight became his passion, and he was willing to take serious risks and pay great costs to see the people of Jerusalem set free from their despair.

I recently finished reading Nelson Mandela's autobiography, *Long Walk to Freedom*. Mandela was so burdened by the injustices faced by black South Africans that he fought the apartheid laws of the white authorities with every ounce of energy he possessed. He and his colleagues pursued the full plethora of strategies offered in the philosophy of nonviolent resistance. Later, he became a leader in the move to a guerrilla resistance movement. This movement primarily focused on sabotage, but it was training for greater activities when Mandela was arrested. At his trial in 1964, Nelson Mandela spoke eloquently and truthfully regarding his activities. He read from his prepared manuscript until he came to the final lines, which he had committed to memory:

> During my lifetime I have dedicated myself to this struggle of the African people. I have fought against white domination and I have fought against black domination. I have cherished the ideal of a democratic and free society in which all persons live together in harmony and with equal opportunities. It is an ideal for which I hope to live for and to achieve. But if needs be, it is an ideal for which I am prepared to die.[7]

Nelson Mandela had a burden that he could not put down, even if it cost him his life. In our text, Nehemiah's burden for his people will not let him go. His burden demands action.

How does Nehemiah take action to help the people of Jerusalem? Nehemiah's first action is prayer, and he opens his prayer with praise. It is important to note that Nehemiah praises God for God's faithfulness in covenant keeping. Covenant refers to a contractual commitment between God and God's people. Arguably, the most well-known covenant in the Old Testament is the Mosaic Covenant. This agreement is between God, who acted as the Deliverer and Provider for the people of Israel through the journey of the exodus, and the people of Israel, who were delivered from bondage and led to the promised land. In Exodus, we read of the consummation of the covenant between God and Israel:

> Moses came and told the people all the words of the LORD and all the ordinances; and all the people answered with one voice, and said, "All the words that the LORD has spoken we will do." And Moses wrote down all the words of the LORD. He rose early in the morning, and built an altar at the foot of the mountain, and set up twelve pillars, corresponding to the twelve tribes of Israel. He sent young men of the people of Israel, who offered burnt offerings and sacrificed oxen as offerings of well-being to the LORD. Moses took half of the blood and put it in basins, and half of the blood he dashed against the altar. Then he took the book of the covenant, and read it in the hearing of the people; and they said, "All that the LORD has spoken we will do, and we will be obedient." Moses took the blood and dashed it on the people, and said, "See the blood of the covenant that the LORD has made with you in accordance with all these words." (Exod 24:3-8)

The people of Israel promised to obey the Law and direction of God. In return, God promised to be the God of Israel, protecting, providing, and prospering them.

The people of Israel, however, developed a pattern of running away from their covenant commitments. Throughout the time of the judges, the united kingdom of Israel, and the divided kingdoms of Israel and Judah, the people turned away from the LORD, only to plead for deliverance in times of direst need. After God's deliverance occurred, the people would return to covenant practice for a time, but eventually, they would resume idolatrous habits. Even the preaching of the prophets did not produce full covenant renewal, so God eventually gave the people over to exile, first the northern kingdom of Israel in 722 BC and then the kingdom of Judah in 587 BC.

Now, almost 100 years after King Cyrus allowed the first group of Jewish exiles to return to Jerusalem, Nehemiah pours out his heart in lament. He recognizes God's faithfulness in always keeping covenant with God's people, and he confesses the covenant faithlessness of himself and his people. Notice, in particular, how Nehemiah confirms that the people of Israel have not kept the decrees and laws given to Moses (v. 7). Nehemiah brings the suffering of God's people before the LORD, but he makes clear that their suffering is the result of their disobedience. Confession is so difficult precisely because people are prone to confessing only when they are able to cast blame on someone else as well. We know children do this: "Yes, I hit my sister, but she hit me first!" We tend to own up to our sin only when the sins of others are pointed out as well. Nehemiah, however, owns his and his people's sin, without shaking a fist at God, the government, the church, or anyone else. Nehemiah's prayer is simple: "God, thank you for keeping covenant with those who follow your commands. Please hear me, even though I, and my people, have broken your covenant over and over again."

Nehemiah, however, is not finished with his prayer. His confession leads him to pray boldly. Nehemiah asks God to honor the core of God's covenant-keeping identity. He urges God to redeem the people when they return to obeying God's laws and decrees. Nehemiah calls on God to embrace the true center of God's great heart: he calls God to love the ones who have wandered away and draw them back.

Redemption is God's heartbeat. Renewal and restoration represent God's deepest longings for all creation. This was the purpose of

God's covenant with Israel: to invite the Israelites into God's redemptive work so "that all the nations of the earth could be blessed." When this covenant plan faltered, God birthed a new covenant through the life, death, and resurrection of God's Son, Jesus, so that all the world could receive the loving invitation into the redeeming life of God, where God and people work together until all things are made new. Nehemiah prays that God will renew this redemptive work in the people of Israel, gathering them anew into a community of grace.

In verse 8, Nehemiah uses an interesting word: "Remember." "Remember" is a popular word in the book of Nehemiah. In this instance, Nehemiah asks God to remember God's own instruction and promises to the people. Obviously, God has not forgotten God's word or promises. Instead, Nehemiah is asking God to reconnect the people of Israel to God's mission, to "remember" them back into God's work of community and redemption. By asking God to remember, Nehemiah also shows that he has remembered his responsibility to God's law and decrees. Nehemiah longs to see people remember and return to covenant obedience even as he has reconnected to God's direction for his life.

Nehemiah prays for God to welcome the people back into the covenant of God's mission. He pleads with God for the restoration of the people. Nehemiah's prayer, however, is not his only response to the burden weighing on his heart for the people of Jerusalem. As we will discover, Nehemiah is a shrewd leader and a clever strategist. He is planning on approaching the king with his concerns about Jerusalem, but he will not do so in a haphazard manner. In fact, it takes Nehemiah roughly four months from when he receives the report from the returnees from Jerusalem before he approaches the king with his requests. During these four months, Nehemiah pours out his heart to the LORD in prayer. He pleads for God to remember God's people. Nehemiah praying for four months before his approach to the king reminds us that even in a crisis, prayer is not merely a reflex but a rhythm. Nehemiah's first and primary response to the suffering in Jerusalem is the development of a pattern of prayer. The days of prayer, however, also lead to a strategy: Nehemiah will approach the king, and this tactic becomes a part of his prayers. We will analyze Nehemiah's approach and conversation with the king in our next session.

Before moving on, however, let us speak a word on behalf of prayerful, strategic action. Too many times, people freeze into a pattern of inertia when they face challenging circumstances.

Sometimes difficult situations at work lead people to malaise instead of initiative. On other occasions, carrying heavy burdens for a prolonged period can lead to apathy and discouragement. There are even times when we want to take action, but the task seems too large to face, so we enter avoidance mode. This is particularly evident when individuals and families face difficult financial or health decisions. It seems easier to avoid the hard budget and exercise conversations, even if they are ultimately good for us. Nehemiah realizes in his times of prayer that he cannot sit still over the plight of the people in Jerusalem. He will have to take action, even though his actions will require great risk.

1. Who, besides a family member, is the first person you would call in the middle of the night if you needed help?

_____

_____

_____

_____

_____

2. What causes you to place great trust in another person? What keeps you from trusting someone?

_____

_____

_____

_____

_____

3. What makes following Jesus easier for a minister than for a layperson? What makes following Jesus easier for a layperson than a minister?

_____

_____

_____

_____

_____

4. Why is Nehemiah deeply saddened by the report from Jerusalem (see Neh 1:3)?

_____

_____

_____

_____

_____

5. What does it mean to live in a covenant relationship with God? How is it the same as/different from living in a covenant relationship like a marriage?

_____

_____

_____

_____

_____

6. What strikes you the most about Nehemiah's prayer in 1:5-10?

_____

_____

_____

_____

_____

7. What role does confession play in your life? In the life of your church?

_____

_____

_____

_____

_____

8. What habits are helpful to your prayer life?

_____

_____

_____

_____

_____

9. Where do you see God doing redeeming work in your life? In your neighborhood? In your world?

_____

_____

_____

_____

_____

10. What burdens are you carrying that are sorrowful to you?

_____

_____

_____

_____

_____

11. What action(s) does God want you take regarding your area of burden?

_____

_____

_____

_____

_____

12. What one area of injustice or concern in our world burdens your class/small group the most? How will you respond to this burden?

_____

_____

_____

_____

_____

Making a Plea . . .
Crafting a Plan

Text: Nehemiah 2

After our first year of marriage, my wife and I moved to a city where we knew no one in order to start a church. We went with the blessing of a local congregation and a variety of denominational partners. We were actually charged with restarting a church plant, which began a few months earlier but was struggling. We announced a restart date, recruited volunteers, and we were off and running within a few months. Pastoring and leading this particular congregation was one of the most deeply satisfying ministry journeys I have experienced. It was also, without a doubt, the hardest work I have ever done.

Two things made pastoring this new church particularly difficult. First, there was no road map. We felt like we were figuring things out every week. Second, I was inexperienced as a leader. We had to face unique challenges as a young congregation, and many times, I had to do things I had never learned to do. There was one task I had to learn quickly: how to ask for money. Our church folks were generous, but a church start rarely pays for its own expenses in the early years. I had to learn to ask regularly, and it was a difficult learning curve.

Early on in our church-starting adventure, I was given the opportunity to talk with the pastor and associate pastor of a large church in our town. I had met the pastor once, and now I was in his office, sharing our young church's mission, strategy, budget, and needs with him. I was terrified. As I reached the end of my presentation, I came to the "ask" part of the conversation. It started like this: "Now, I know you know that all the plans and dreams in this presentation cost money. I hate to ask you . . . ." The pastor cut me off.

"Hold it right there," he ordered. "You have shared with me for the past thirty minutes what God is doing in your new congregation.

You have told me about baptizing adults, dreams for new ministry, and opportunities for our church to be involved. You have told me that God is at work and that you see new opportunities for doing God's work. Is all this true?"

"Absolutely," I said, a little taken aback.

He replied, "Then do not ever again for the rest of your ministry apologize for asking people to give to God's work that will change lives. Let them determine what the Holy Spirit is asking them to do, but never apologize for asking people to give to God's mission."

I left the meeting with the promise of a generous contribution. The church became a powerful partner with our church, but the biggest gift of the meeting was the charge of the wise pastor: "Never apologize for asking people to give to God's mission." He was right.

The context of our Scripture text is that Nehemiah pondered his grief for nearly four months. Nehemiah listened for what God is calling him to do, and as much as he wants to shrink back from the challenge, Nehemiah must ask the king not only to let him go to Jerusalem but also to provide for his journey and absence. Even though Nehemiah enjoys the trust of the king, asking an absolute ruler to relinquish items from his treasury for a mission many miles away is no small matter. Asking for money can always alter a relationship.

Nehemiah's trepidation in coming to Artaxerxes, however, may have an additional source. In Ezra 4:18-22 (covered in session 3 above), a letter attributed to King Artaxerxes is delivered to Rehum, the commanding officer of Persian forces in Samaria. In this letter, the king orders the troops in Samaria to go to Jerusalem to stop a wall-rebuilding project that is in progress. In fact, Artaxerxes tells his soldiers to "not neglect this matter. Why let this threat grow in detriment of the royal interests?" (Ezra 4:22, NIV). At this command of Artaxerxes, Persian soldiers marched into Jerusalem and "compelled [the Jews] by force to stop" (Ezra 4:23, NIV). It stands to reason that these events occurred before Nehemiah went to Artaxerxes to talk about the conditions in Jerusalem. In his meeting with the king, Nehemiah will not only have to ask for a leave of absence from his present work and for resources from the king's treasury; his requests will also require the king to reverse his prior policies on Jerusalem. No wonder Nehemiah spends four months in prayer and planning. He knows the delicacy of what he must ask the king.

At the beginning of Nehemiah 2, the author portrays the conversation between Nehemiah and King Artaxerxes as extemporaneous.

Nehemiah is burdened with sadness, and the king inquires about his sorrow. Here, Nehemiah has a choice: he can simply gloss over how he feels, or he can sense in the king's question an open opportunity provided by the Spirit of God. It is possible that Nehemiah would have preferred a planned moment where he could organize his PowerPoint slides, but he has pondered this presentation in prayer and planning for a number of months. So, since he has the king's attention, he plunges forward, telling the king how he is afflicted with sadness due to the state of Jerusalem. In response, the king asks, "What do you want?"

Nehemiah does not answer the question with a shrug of his shoulders or a response like, "Well, you are smarter than me. What would you suggest?" A request to a leader, elected official, boss, parent, or anyone in a position of power is foolish without a plan. Nehemiah offers a silent word of prayer, which is merely an overflow of his months of praying, and he charges forward with a well-rehearsed outline of his needs. He asks King Artaxerxes to send him to Jerusalem to rebuild the city. Notice that he does not merely ask to rebuild the wall. Nehemiah's vision is much larger. He wants to see Jerusalem whole and prosperous under the leadership of God. After the king accedes to Nehemiah's appointment to Jerusalem, Nehemiah continues his requests. He asks the king for a letter of safe passage through all the lands he will enter on the way to Jerusalem. King Artaxerxes grants this request and even gives him an armed escort to protect his travel party. Finally, Nehemiah asks the king to provide wood for the temple gates and for his residence as the governor of Judah. The king shows great generosity in agreeing to all of Nehemiah's appeals.

It is tempting to look to Nehemiah for fundraising lessons, but Nehemiah knows the real reason the king is so generous with him. Nehemiah 2:8b (NIV) reads, "And because the gracious hand of my God was upon me, the king granted my requests." Nehemiah understands his presentation skills do not convince the king to reverse course on his Jerusalem rebuilding policy. Rather, God's work in the heart of Artaxerxes leads to the favorable outcome.

King Artaxerxes' response to Nehemiah continues the theme of God working through unexpected people in Ezra-Nehemiah. We have noted how the writer of Ezra attributed Cyrus's decision permitting the return of the Jewish exiles to the work of God in his heart. In Ezra 6, the decree of King Darius allows the work on the temple to continue under the leadership of Zerubbabel and the prophet Haggai and Zechariah. Ezra 6:14 states that the people finished building the temple under the commands of God and the decrees of Cyrus, Darius, and Artaxerxes. Clearly, the writer views the decrees of the Persian rulers as part of the fulfillment of God's commands concerning the Israelites.

King Artaxerxes, in fact, furthers the plans of God on two different occasions. First, he sends Ezra to Jerusalem to assess the religious practices of the people and to teach them the laws of God. His goal is to foster the religious reformation of the people of Jerusalem. Then, in our current text, Artaxerxes agrees to send Nehemiah to promote the civic and long-term economic sustainability of Jerusalem. God uses Artaxerxes to usher in two complementary streams of reform in Jerusalem, even though he at one point actually halted the rebuilding of the city. It is clear that one primary theme of Ezra-Nehemiah is that God works through people to accomplish God's purposes, even when the people in question are not members of God's community. For our application, we must learn to notice where God is at work outside the walls of the church. God is working for the redemption of all creation in places and people we do not expect.

After receiving permission from the king, Nehemiah journeys to Jerusalem. Nehemiah is a savvy, determined leader. He knows his first few days with the people will set the tone for his years of leading them. In the first three days of Nehemiah's stay in Jerusalem, he makes three critical leadership decisions. First, he does not immediately share his wall-building agenda with the leaders of the community. He does not arrive and announce grand plans for the redevelopment of Jerusalem. He does not come to this place, which as far as we know he has never seen, and hand out an immediate agenda without the citizens' input. There are no banners, rallies, slogans, or festivals designed to hype the crowds. Instead, Nehemiah arrives, rests, and waits. He refuses to announce a direction without having his facts clear and message prepared.

Second, Nehemiah assesses the condition of the wall on his own rather than relying on secondhand information. After three days of getting his bearings, Nehemiah heads off in the middle of the night to examine the walls of Jerusalem. Why does he go in the middle of the night? He wants privacy and discretion. It is his intention to make his own assessment of the condition of the walls and gates of the city. He will not encourage the people to rebuild the walls without knowing the full weight of the task he is proposing. Furthermore, he will not base his plans on secondhand knowledge. He makes his own investigation of the situation without quizzing or blaming the leaders of the people. He goes with only a few trusted friends because he does not want to listen to excuses, blame, complaints, or reasons that the project is not feasible. Nehemiah takes fresh eyes to the scene and makes his own judgments.

Nehemiah is a careful planner. It is not hard to imagine that, as he examines the southern portion of the broken walls and gates of Jerusalem, he takes copious mental notes. Perhaps he notes the sections of the wall that need the most work, figures the amount of timber required for a particular gate, and even thinks through which sections need attention first. All of this information is integrated into his plan, not only for engaging the people in the work but also for the particulars of the work itself. He will soon have to face the leaders of the people and unveil his direction to them, and he wants all of his information ready for the upcoming conversation.

Nehemiah's initial silence and his desire to formulate his own observations regarding the apathy of the people and the condition of the wall are significant leadership decisions. In fact, how a leader begins a new project or position with a group of apathetic, worn-down people often determines the success or failure of the endeavor. Patrick Lencioni, a well-known developer of leadership teams, once wrote a fable about a fictitious CEO named Kathryn. She was given the role of CEO in a company struggling with stagnation, mean-spiritedness among team members, and a general sense of apathy. Thrust into this desperate leadership situation, Kathryn's initial strategy provoked surprise and second-guessing:

> If the executives at Decision Tech had any doubts about Kathryn when her hiring was first announced—and they did—they were even more concerned after their new leader's first two weeks on the job. It wasn't that Kathryn did anything controversial or misplaced. It was that she did almost nothing at all. Aside from a brief reception on the first day and subsequent interviews with her direct reports, Kathryn spent almost all of her time walking the halls, chatting with staff members, and silently observing as many meetings as she could find time to attend. And perhaps most controversial of all, she actually asked Jeff Shanley [founder and CEO of the company] to continue leading the weekly executive staff meetings, where she just listened and took notes.[8]

The CEO in Lencioni's writing follows an approach similar to Nehemiah's. Nehemiah's decision not to reveal his vision too soon and to assess the situation himself leads to a compelling initial call to the leaders of Jerusalem. Notice how Nehemiah begins his persuasion to the leaders of the people: "Then I said to them, 'You see the trouble we are in, how Jerusalem lies in ruins with its gates burned. Come, let us rebuild the wall of Jerusalem, so that we may no longer suffer disgrace'" (Neh 2:17). Notice that he says the trouble "we" are in, rather than the trouble "you" are in. Nehemiah is careful to include himself in the destiny of the people. People buy in to a leader's plan when the plan represents a community investment rather than an outside agenda. Nehemiah makes it clear that he is rooting himself in the city, that the issues of the people will affect him as well. He is a community member, not an absentee overseer.

Finally, Nehemiah's third leadership decision is his refusal to blame the people and leaders for the current condition of the city. Of course, Nehemiah knows the situation and trouble of the city better than anyone else in the room. He has examined the wall firsthand with fresh eyes, whereas the people have grown comfortable with the decimated conditions. Familiarity with poor conditions often makes people accept and even ignore those conditions. Nehemiah sees the problems and neglect of the people clearly, and yet he refuses to assign blame for past failures and poor decisions. People are rarely motivated by blame, and when they are, the motivation rarely lasts long. Nehemiah calls the leaders to action by helping them focus on their collective, present problems rather than pointing a finger at them for permitting the problems to persist.

Of course, the leaders of Jerusalem know they are in disgrace. They had even prepared to repair the gates and walls themselves years earlier, only to have their work forcibly stopped by the command of Artaxerxes. Certainly, many of the leaders would have agreed that Nehemiah's course of action was right, but perhaps they quickly returned to the line we often hear in our churches, schools, companies, and even government: "We tried that before, and it didn't work." In order to overcome these sentiments of opposition, Nehemiah saves his most powerful point for last: "I told them that the hand of my God had been gracious upon me, and also the words that the king had spoken to me" (2:18).

Nehemiah does not merely tell the people that God has called him to lead in the rebuilding of the city of Jerusalem. Instead, he tells the people that God has called him to lead Jerusalem forward, and he gives concrete examples of how God has worked through his own circumstances to facilitate the rebuilding process. Nehemiah tells them how God led him before Artaxerxes and also led the king to respond favorably to Nehemiah's mission to Jerusalem. The leaders of Jerusalem recognize the hand of God in Nehemiah's story, and they resolve to fully join and support the work of rebuilding the wall.

There are many conversations in books, articles, sermons, blogs, and podcasts regarding how followers of Jesus can connect with the "nones,"[9] members of other religious groups, and people who have disengaged from the Christianity of our culture. As church membership declines and the United States grows more secular, we wonder, "How do we let others know that Jesus loves them?" Nehemiah gives us a simple, two-part pattern to consider and practice. First, listen and befriend people who believe differently than you do. As Nehemiah scoured the walls of Jerusalem and listened to the happenings of the city before he spoke, we too should collect and give careful attention to the stories and journeys of those who do not believe as we do. Only then do we earn the opportunity to proceed to the next step: telling the story of how God in Jesus Christ is at work in our lives. We do not invite others to church programs, attempting to convert them with slick arguments or presentations; we simply tell our stories. In the sharing of stories between friends, the Holy Spirit does God's work, and both friends are changed and respected in the process. Stories of God at work are the best truths we have to share with others.

1. Share the story of a time when you had to ask for something from another person and were nervous about the request. How did you prepare for the conversation?

_____

_____

_____

_____

_____

2. When you face a problem or a difficult situation, are you the kind of person who "jumps right in," or do you research and assess before moving forward? What are the advantages and disadvantages of each approach?

_____

_____

_____

_____

_____

3. Why was Nehemiah so successful in his requests to Artaxerxes?

_____

_____

_____

_____

_____

4. What do you think of Nehemiah's strategy of being silent and assessing the condition of the walls of Jerusalem by himself? What would you have done differently?

_____

_____

_____

_____

_____

5. Describe the leadership characteristics you see in Nehemiah. Which ones are the most important to you?

_____

_____

_____

_____

_____

6. When you face a difficult conversation with someone else, how do you help the person know that you are truly hearing and understanding his or her perspective?

_____

_____

_____

_____

_____

7. What does it take to jolt you out of an apathetic approach to areas of disrepair in your life?

_____

_____

_____

_____

_____

8. What is one area of disrepair in your life that you would like to start rebuilding? Now that you have identified it, what next steps will you take?

_____

_____

_____

_____

_____

Making a Plea . . . Crafting a Plan

Overcoming Obstacles,
Outlasting Critics

Session

Text: Nehemiah 4

The crux of Nehemiah 2 is that Nehemiah calls the leaders of Jerusalem to work on rebuilding the wall, and the people take up the task. They commit themselves to the work fully, and Nehemiah 3 details how the people are assigned to their roles of responsibility in the project. It is tempting to see chapters 2 and 3 as the complete victory of forward momentum for the city redevelopment effort that God planted in the heart of Nehemiah. Nehemiah 2, however, actually offers two ominous signs for the future of the wall-building enterprise. In 2:10 and 2:19-20, we discover that Sanballat, the governor of Samaria, and Tobiah, another area official, are not happy with the wall-building efforts. They see Nehemiah as a rival and immediately attempt to join the work of repairing the wall in order to exercise control over the situation. Nehemiah rebuffs their seemingly sincere effort at cooperation, which diffuses the immediate threat. Sanballat and Tobiah, however, have only begun their opposition strategies.

In Nehemiah 4, these two take up active opposition to the wall renovation efforts of the people of Jerusalem. Of course, Sanballat and Tobiah could have chosen another course. They could have offered neighborly council and protection for the project. They could have come to Nehemiah in trust and friendship since all three of them have been appointed to their positions by the king. Instead, they choose the route of mistrust and political posturing. They worry that a rebuilt Jerusalem will decrease their influence and power, so they mock the rebuilding effort.

In truth, mocking is an understatement. Sanballat and Tobiah ridicule the construction practices and the character of the people. They scream insults, laugh at God's people in front of their advisers and troops, and use every verbal insult possible to berate them into submission. They seek to remind the people of their failures and to convince them that they do not have the skill, resolve, or aptitude to finish such a difficult task. Sanballat and Tobiah assume that the Jews will cower in the face of derision as they have in the past. They figure that the Jewish people will simply acquiesce into the forlorn and defeated posture of a broken people.

We do not like to admit it, but our words have the power to beat people into submission. We often say that "sticks and stones may break my bones but words will never hurt me," but it is rarely true. Words can wound, whether in verbal or written form. Perhaps this is why the author of Proverbs urges his readers to speak righteous words (see Prov 10:19-20 and 11:12), the Apostle Paul reacts strongly to news that the church in Corinth is engaged in sinful behaviors including gossip and slander (see 2 Cor 12:20), and James talks so passionately about the dangers of the tongue (see Jas 3, esp. vv. 9-12). Throughout the Bible, God's followers are warned regarding the dangers of derisive, mean-spirited words. The teaching is clear: people who have committed their lives to following Jesus do not wound others physically; neither are we permitted to bludgeon others with our words, even if those whom we insult are absent. Followers of Jesus are called to a life of encouragement, or, in the words of Paul, to "not let any unwholesome talk come out of your mouths, but only what is helpful for building others up according to their needs, that it may benefit those who listen" (Eph 4:29, NIV). The Bible takes malicious words seriously, and so must we.

The strategy of Sanballat and Tobiah is simple: they will shame the people of Jerusalem into abandoning their work. This tactic has worked on other occasions. In fact, it has worked so well that Nehemiah faced a beaten, broken people when he arrived, a people who gave up on the call to redevelop their city. They have acquiesced to the bullying and belittling of their neighbors.

Unfortunately, too many people still believe it is appropriate to belittle or coerce people in order to achieve their goals. Sometimes it happens in the boardroom when the intimidating CEO rains down derision and fire on an employee in order to avoid his own fears of failure. It happens when a mother shames her adult daughter through guilt trips and phrases of manipulation. It happens in high schools when one teen texts an ugly rumor or picture about another, and the subject of the gossip must endure heckling on social media outlets for an extended period. It happens in churches when pastors and staff members are berated in private, when choir members talk negatively about those who do not come to rehearsal, or when the church "in crowd" laughs about a fringe church attender rather than inviting him or her to connect deeper to the network of the congregation. People use words to wound for a variety of reasons, but whatever the reason, it is wrong, and all too often our harsh words leave permanent scars. Finally, berating words permeated the 2016 presidential election cycle and left our nation polarized and bitter.

The people of Jerusalem, however, are not cowered by the insults and derisive comments of Sanballat, Tobiah, and their cohorts. In fact, they do not offer any response to these verbal attacks other than continued efforts at rebuilding the wall. Nehemiah responds by asking God to hear the insults of their attackers and to remember how the antagonists have treated the people of Jerusalem.

When it is clear that the people of Jerusalem are not going to give up in the face of verbal taunts and insults, Sanballat and Tobiah grow angry. They threaten the people of Jerusalem with military intervention. If the people will not stop their work because of verbal abuse, they will face attack and annihilation: "And our enemies said, 'They will not know or see anything before we come upon them and kill them and stop the work'" (Neh 4:11). The threats of physical violence from their enemies escalate the concerns of Nehemiah and the people. Certainly, insults are painful, but an actual physical attack would derail progress and harm lives. At this time, Jerusalem does not have an organized army, and clearly they did not have a prepared and fortified defense perimeter. They are sitting ducks. If the work is to continue, Nehemiah will have to devise a way to counteract the military might of the neighboring regions.

Unfortunately, the physical threats of Sanballat and Tobiah are not the biggest obstacles facing Nehemiah and the people of Jerusalem. The larger issue is the people themselves: they have lost their resolve. "Meanwhile, the people in Judah said, 'The strength of the laborers is giving out, and there is so much rubble that we cannot rebuild the wall'" (4:10). The people have worked hard and seen extensive progress. Now, however, they are worn down and ready to quit. Certainly, they are exhausted because manual labor is hard work, especially without the aid of power tools, forklifts, and other modern construction equipment. There are, however, additional explanations for their depleted energy.

First, enthusiasm for the project has decreased. It is natural when a new venture begins for participants to respond with enthusiasm and fervor. It is also normal for enthusiasm to wane as people settle into the day-to-day drudgery of the project. If the leader is not careful, lowered enthusiasm can lead to stalled momentum, disinterest, fatigue, and discouragement. Clearly, the momentum for the wall-rebuilding project has faded. Nehemiah must address this fatigue and take action to re-engage the people.

Next, progress on the wall has slowed. In any large construction project, there are points where the pace decreases and progress is nearly invisible. These moments are fertile ground for discouragement and discontent. The apparent lack of progress feeds into the waning enthusiasm, and both issues threaten the momentum of the project.

Finally, the people are not only physically exhausted but also emotionally depleted. They have moved from a stolid existence to a furious work pace in a short amount of time. Rapid change takes a toll on people even in the best of circumstances. They have endured insults and derisive remarks from neighbors. They even face the threat of armed attacks against them at any moment. The confluence of stressors and anxiety drains the people of their emotional will. Nehemiah faces the most serious leadership challenge of his life: in the face of threats from outsiders and the exhaustion of insiders, how will he inspire the people to push forward?

Let's begin by noticing what Nehemiah does not do in addressing the obstacles and critics. He does not ignore them. He does not minimize the pressures of multiple crises that threaten to derail the wall-rebuilding effort. He does not chastise the people for their lack of faith in the face of danger or embrace the tactics of their enemy and attempt to bully the people to continue working. Furthermore, he does not retreat or give up. Nehemiah knows completing the wall depends on the people taking action to overcome their barriers and critics, but he also knows they must take the right action! In the same way Nehemiah carefully considered the state of the wall, he now ponders the best way to reinvigorate the people in their wall-building calling. Nehemiah does not make a haphazard decision. Instead, he makes carefully considered, decisive moves in the face of the crisis.

Before analyzing Nehemiah's responses to the obstacles and critics, we need to appreciate the significance of decisive moments. Nehemiah faces a critical, perhaps *the* critical, moment of his time as the governor of Judah. These moments of critical decision-making happen for all of us, and we often have little specific preparation time to make good judgments. The truth, however, is that the courses of our lives, and the lives of those we lead and serve, are determined by the quality of our decision-making, particularly in vitally important matters. Noel Tichy and Warren Bennis explain the importance of judgment in this way:

> Throughout our lives, each of us makes thousands of judgment calls. . . . The measure of our success is the sum of all these judgment calls. How many good ones did we make? And more important, did we make good ones about the things that really mattered? Our ability to exercise good judgment determines the quality of our individual lives. And, as we rise to positions of leadership, the importance and consequences of our judgment calls are magnified exponentially by their increasing impact on the lives of others. The cumulative effect of leaders' judgment calls determines the success or failure of their organizations.[10]

Obviously, Tichy and Bennis write from a secular perspective, so the importance of prayer and the Holy Spirit in decision-making are not addressed, but their main point is still appropriate for followers of Jesus: good judgment, particularly in the major decisions of life, leads to better living. It is imperative, therefore, that people prepare themselves in regular time to make good decisions when major moments of decision-making arrive. As we have seen, Nehemiah is adept at prayerful planning and preparation. His prayers and meditations are his foundation for the decisions he must make to lead the people of Jerusalem in spite of obstacles and critics.

Nehemiah's first judgment pertaining to the threats of Sanballat and Tobiah results in a reengineering of the construction process. Up to this point, all the people in Jerusalem were working on the wall. In response to the threats of physical violence, however, Nehemiah issues new assignments. Some people continue working on the wall, but others take spears, swords, bows, and shields and stand in the gaps and low places of the wall. If enemies attack to disrupt the project, Jerusalem is ready. This standing militia ensures that the work will continue, even in the event of a surprise attack.

In addition to the standing militia, the workers alter their routine. Now, material runners will carry their materials in one hand and a sword in the other. Likewise, the workers on the wall keep their swords at all times. Even though these changes mean the workers carry less material and that the swords slow their work, this is acceptable in order to protect the people and the project.

I love the image of "working with one hand and carrying a sword with another" (Neh 4:17). My appreciation for this image is not due to a violent disposition or a crusading approach to Christian living in the world. Rather, the image of "working with one hand and carrying a sword in the other" speaks to the spiritual vigilance followers of Jesus must carry in our culture. We diligently love, pray, worship, connect with our neighbors, and practice hospitality in order to participate in the mission of God. We also, however, must battle injustice. When payday lenders take advantage of the poor in our cities, we must stand up against the injustice. When public schools are mismanaged, schools in poorer neighborhoods are underserved, and children are the causalities of poor educational practice, we must take action. When young girls and boys are pressed into the sex trade around the world and in our own cities due to the greed and selfishness of predators, we must fight against this injustice. Following Jesus is a calling to the work of love, but love is not passive. When love sees injustice, it is compelled to advocate and act. Like the soldiers of Nehemiah's militia, we are called by love to "stand in the gap" against the brokenness and injustice in our culture.

Nehemiah, however, does not simply retool the building project as his answer to the obstacles and critics. He recasts the vision for the entire venture. He calls the people to remember the calling they have received. More important, he reminds them of the faithfulness and power of the God who called them forward to rebuild the wall. He reminds them of the almighty power of God, who will not leave them even if they do face attacks at the hands of their neighbors. Finally, Nehemiah exhorts the people to action in the name of God: "Do not give up," he cries. "If need be, stand up and fight for your families, homes, and fields. Do not give in to fear, but stand up under the power and might of God and move forward in finishing this wall." The people are encouraged by Nehemiah's words, and, in spite of daunting opposition, they keep working, knowing God will fight with them if a battle is necessary. Nehemiah's decisions to retool the wall-building process and to recast the vision for rebuilding the wall prove the right judgments for a fearful and tenuous situation.

One of the most essential tasks of leadership in the church is regularly reminding the people of what God has called them to do. Church leaders must regularly "recast the vision" because, in the midst of routines and relationships, we lose perspective and energy. We lose sight of the mission God has given. In the face of the daunting realities of church life in the United States, we even lose hope. We need Nehemiah leaders—laypersons and clergy who stand in front of us and lead the charge, remind us of what we are called to do, and exhort us not to give in to fear, anxiety, blaming, exhaustion, discouragement, or anything else that distracts us from the power and calling of God.

1. Describe a time when you were bullied as a child. What emotions do you remember the most? Do you think adults bully other adults? Why or why not?

_____

_____

_____

_____

_____

2. What is the most exhausting experience you have ever had? How did you recover?

_____

_____

_____

_____

_____

3. What are the "outside" obstacles that Nehemiah and the people faced? How do you face similar obstacles in your own life?

_____

_____

_____

_____

_____

4. What "inside" obstacles did Nehemiah and the people face? How do you face these?

_____

_____

_____

_____

_____

5. When are you most prone to physical exhaustion and/or mental fatigue? How do you rest and recover?

_____

_____

_____

_____

_____

6. When are you most prone to discouragement? To fear? What do you do about this?

_____

_____

_____

_____

_____

7. Describe the actions Nehemiah took to protect the people from an outside attack. Which action was the most important? Why?

_____

_____

_____

_____

_____

8. How are you affected by what other people say about you? How do you handle it when someone speaks negatively about you?

_____

_____

_____

_____

_____

9. How do you "get over" discouragement? How do you handle your fear?

_____

_____

_____

_____

_____

10. One of the best ways to overcome discouragement is to practice authentic encouragement. What do you do to encourage others? Would you describe your church or small group as people of encouragement? Why or why not?

_____

_____

_____

_____

_____

11. Is there any "retooling" that needs to take place in your walk with God? If so, what needs to change? How can God and your church help you "retool" areas of your spirituality?

_____

_____

_____

_____

_____

12. What inspires you to keep moving in doing God's work in your community? What, or who, inspires you to grow deeper in your walk with God?

_____
_____
_____
_____
_____

Conviction, Celebration, and Worship

Text: Nehemiah 8

In beginning a study of Nehemiah 8–10, one notices that the story of Nehemiah 1–7 does not connect well with chapters 8–10. In fact, if one reads 1–7 and continues on with chapters 11–13, the chronology of the story makes more sense. Nehemiah 8 presents perhaps the greatest chronological challenge in the Ezra-Nehemiah volume. After all, the completion of the wall-rebuilding project is reported in Nehemiah 6:15-19, and chapter 7 describes how Nehemiah organizes the temple hierarchy and records another list of returning exiles. It stands to reason that a celebration commemorating the completed wall would appear in chapter 8, but the prelude to the wall dedication does not begin until chapter 11, with the wall dedication ceremony coming in chapter 12. Clearly, something is out of sequence in chapters 8–10.

The lack of chronological continuity of these chapters is further underscored by their content. In chapter 8, Ezra returns to the forefront. He is depicted reading the Law to the people, almost as if it is the inaugural moment of his Law-teaching ministry to the people. Since Nehemiah is present at this occasion, it is puzzling that it took Ezra thirteen years to introduce the Law to the full assembly of the people. Obviously, Ezra could have read the Law on other occasions, but the lack of knowledge of the Law by the people and the deep sense of conviction they experienced could point to a lack of familiarity with the Law itself. Whatever the reasoning, two points regarding Nehemiah 8–10 are important for this work: (1) The chronological relationship between the persons of Ezra and Nehemiah is impossible to describe with absolute certainty, and (2) Nehemiah 8–10 is inserted for its theological perspective rather than for establishing a linear chronology of the years of Ezra and Nehemiah.[11]

As you study Nehemiah 8–10, do your best to let the chronology questions fade into the background. The Bible is not written as a chronological history; rather, it is theological history, telling us the story of what God is like and how God is active in loving and redeeming creation. These chapters are placed into the context of the whole of Nehemiah to speak the truths of God's story regarding the people of Jerusalem to all generations. It is our task, with the Holy Spirit's guidance, to ponder why these chapters are included in this place and what they have to teach us about following Jesus. Thankfully, there is much for us to ruminate over on both accounts.

As noted above, Ezra's reading of the Law does not immediately follow the completion of the wall. The writer includes the reading of the Law and the corresponding worship of the people at this point to emphasize the interconnectivity between the redevelopment of Jerusalem and the renewal of the people's connection with God. The renewal of the city and the revival of the people's spiritual commitment are not independent occurrences. They are woven together by the power and provision of God. The writer emphasizes the completion of the wall as an act of faithful obedience to Yahweh by placing a corporate worship gathering, centered on obedience to the Law of God, after the details related to the wall's completion. This completion is the result of faithfulness to God's commands rather than the people's construction prowess.

The centerpiece of the great assembly described in Ezra 8:1-8 is the reading of the Law of Moses, likely the Torah, the first five books of the Old Testament. The Law was read only sporadically, if at all during the exile; and, in the years between the return of the first exiles and Ezra's arrival, the Law was neglected and then lost. This explains King Artaxerxes' reasoning for sending Ezra to evaluate the religious practices of Jerusalem and to teach them the laws of their faith. On this occasion, Ezra reads the book of the Law from morning until noon, and the Levites are actually out in the assembly explaining and instructing the listeners so they understand the words they are hearing.

As Paul would echo approximately 500 years later, the Law leads to an awareness of sin (see Rom 7:7). As the people realize the depths of their sinfulness, they begin to weep. Verse 9 tells us that the people mourn and weep under the weight of the conviction brought about by the reading of the law of the LORD. Ezra and Nehemiah, however, tell the people to stop weeping! Of course, these prophets are not making light of or excusing the sin of the people. It is due to their leadership that the people are present in the assembly to hear the Law in the first place. Why do they rush around quieting the sobs of the congregation?

Ezra and Nehemiah are aware of how easily one moves from experiencing the conviction of God to falling into the abyss of self-abusing guilt. So, before the people move from conviction to self-pity, Ezra and Nehemiah intercede to remind them of God's goodness and grace. They remind the people that the day is for celebrating God's response to their sin, which is the grace of a fresh start in a reborn city with a new temple, wall, and opportunity to recommit themselves to God's law. Therefore, Ezra and Nehemiah compel the people to celebrate the joy of the LORD and to include even the poorest in this banquet of grace.

Present-day followers of Jesus can learn many truths from the Law-reading worship assembly in Nehemiah 8 and its results. For the sake of brevity, I will confine my observations to two. First, most American followers of Jesus struggle with developing joy. If you look in many American churches, and even in many American church worship services, authentic joy is difficult to find. Christians are called to embody a life of joy. We are set free from sin and have the opportunity to live, regardless of our circumstances, in the freedom and love of God in Christ Jesus. This does not mean all of our circumstances make us happy; instead, it means that even when our circumstances are damaging and painful, we have an inner reservoir of the peace and joy of Jesus to sustain us. C. S. Lewis wrote, "Joy is the serious business of heaven."[12] If joy is indeed heaven's business, Christ-followers must endeavor to make joy prevalent "on earth as it is in heaven."

Unfortunately, many Christians are distracted from developing joy in their lives and bringing joy to their neighborhoods. So many Christians are mired deep in bitterness, resentment, defensiveness, complaint, anxiety, exhaustion, and judgmentalism. We are called to exude generous joy in worship and ordinary living, and yet we allow the circumstances of our lives to deprive us of the privilege of joyful living. John Ortberg says it this way:

> The Bible puts joy in the nonoptional [sic] category. Joy is a command. Joylessness is a serious sin, one that religious people are particularly prone to indulge in. It may be the sin most readily tolerated by the church . . . . How often have people misunderstood God because they attributed to him the grim judgmental,

defensive, soul-wearying spirit of many who claim to be his followers?[13]

Joy is not a by-product of our lives as followers of Jesus; it is a foundational characteristic of our identity in Christ.

The people's response to the reading of the Law, however, offers one other lesson for present-day American Christ-followers: we must embrace the discipline of lament. Put another way, we must learn to weep and mourn over the wounds and injustices of our world. This seems contradictory to the preceding challenge of cultivating the joy of the Lord, but in actuality, developing our capacity for lamentation increases our capability for joy.

The notion of joy couching itself in affliction, suffering, and sorrow is central to the Christian faith. The core story of the resurrection of Jesus on Easter Sunday is only possible against the backdrop of lament and sorrow found on Good Friday. The juxtaposition of sorrow and joy found in the death and resurrection of Jesus carries over into the early Christian movement. Paul, in his second Corinthian letter, praises the faith of the churches of Macedonia by saying, "In the midst of a very severe trial, their overflowing joy and their extreme poverty welled up in rich generosity" (2 Cor 8:2, NIV). In the book of James, the writer challenges his audience with these words: "My brothers and sisters, whenever you face trials of any kind, consider it nothing but joy, because you know that the testing of your faith produces endurance; and let endurance have its full effect, so that you may be mature and complete, lacking in nothing" (Jas 1:2-4).

Enduring and lamenting sorrow and suffering leads to the development and practice of joy. This is the evidence of the New Testament and of the Psalms, where many of the Psalms of Lament conclude with a promise of praise or a resolve to return to the ways of God. Even in the deep mourning and grief of the five poems of Lamentations, there is a moment of light in Lamentations 3:21-27 that looks briefly toward hoping in the LORD. In a real sense, then, suffering and lament are long, desolate roads to joy and hope. As the fictional Edmond Dantes stated in *The Count of Monte Cristo,*

> As for you, Morrel, this is the whole secret of my behavior towards you; there is neither happiness nor misfortune in this world, there is only the comparison between one state and another, nothing more. Only someone who has suffered the deepest misfortune is

capable of experiencing the heights of felicity. Maximilien, you must needs have wished to die, to know how good it is to live.[14]

If the experience of deep grief has the capacity to lead people to joy and hope, then how do people mourn well? How can followers of Jesus lament like the writers of Jeremiah, the Psalms of Lament, and the people listening to Ezra read the Law? How do we lament well?

Lamenting is pouring out pain to God in prayer. Many times, followers of Jesus are taught that praying sad prayers is a sign of faithlessness, weakness, or selfishness. Nothing could be further from the truth. God wants to hear what we are feeling. We do not need to sterilize our thoughts, sadness, and pain into theologically appropriate frameworks in order to pour out our hearts to God. Instead, we spew, vent, cry, and, if necessary, rage. However we carry our laments to God, there is simply one rule: our crying out must be authentic and raw. When we hurt, God is big enough to handle our questions, fears, spasms of grief, frustration, and tears. Prayers of lament are the prayers of the broken.

We can also join in the mourning and lament of the people listening to Ezra read the Law of God. Whenever I come face to face with the call of Jesus—with the commands to love my enemies and forgive those who are deceitful to me—and then read through the fruit of the Spirit Paul calls me to cultivate as a follower of Jesus, I am overwhelmed at how far I have to go. I am humbled by the lack of love in my heart, the resentment I struggle to release, and the lack of peace I feel as I move through my days. I am not immersed in unhealthy guilt, but I sense ever more my ongoing need for grace. So I lament: I mourn over the areas of my life I have worked to reform that still need renovation, weep to myself over my struggle to love people who disagree with me or hurt me, and shudder at the times where I have treated others poorly. In these moments of lament and repentance over my own sin, I feel again the touch of the One who forgives my sin and leads my life, and my lament moves to joy and peace as I step forward in the arms of God's grace, which is the only real way any of us step forward at all.

One final word about lament: we must weep and wail over the injustice and brokenness of our world. Nehemiah wept, mourned, and lamented to the core of his being the brokenness of Jerusalem and the corporate sin of the people that brought them into such a condition. What are you mourning as you move through your days?

Are you weeping over a broken marriage or difficult parenting situation? Are you mourning your own vocational angst or future goals? Is there a community issue or concern that leads you to brokenness and lament? Is there an injustice that keeps you awake at night, which unleashes in the depths of your spirit a gut-wrenching cry in God's direction? As Nehemiah wept over Jerusalem, as Jesus later lamented over Jerusalem, we too are called to lament the brokenness and pain of our lives and world before God. We grieve fully, but also as people fully assured of God's love, presence, and ability to turn our "mourning into dancing." As 1 Thessalonians reminds us, followers of Jesus grieve with hope.

The lament, joy, and feasting the people embraced at the reading of the Law moves to a new day of worship. There is a rhythm of worship taking place with conviction and celebration over the reintegration of the practice of the Law into the community. The people begin their renewal of participation in the laws of God through the practice of the Feast of Tabernacles (also called the Feast of Ingathering), which God instructed the people of Israel to observe (see Exod 23:16, 34:22; Num 23:33-49). Like the original returnees decades before, the remnant under Ezra and Nehemiah worshiped God through celebrating God's provision in the Festival of Tabernacles (see Ezra 3:4 and session 2 above). The people built booths for themselves and reflected on the time their ancestors lived in the desert as God led them out of bondage in Egypt and to the promised land of Canaan. The booths reminded the people of the days when their ancestors lived in the desert for forty years, without any permanent dwelling. They pondered the faithfulness of God to their ancestors, and they reflected on the promises and care of God in bringing them back to Jerusalem from exile. They celebrated the festival with renewed gratitude and joy as they listened each day to Ezra read from the Law. In fact, Nehemiah 8:17 reports that the celebration of the festival was epic in its fervor, because they celebrated with greater intensity than any time since the days of Joshua. The people have moved from hearing the Law of God to observing the Law of God.

The move to observing the Festival of Tabernacles is a significant step forward in the spiritual renewal of the people. They are not only listening to and sensing the conviction of the law of God but also transforming their behavior as a community according to the law of God. The Festival of Tabernacles was an eight-day festival where people remembered the faithfulness of God to their ancestors in the wilderness and celebrated God's faithfulness in providing crops and water for their survival. For the people who have returned to Jerusalem from Susa and other areas of the Persian Empire, their sustenance is not guaranteed. They have to plant new crops, establish new homes, and rebuild the wall for their security. Participating in the Festival of Tabernacles is a significant act of worship because they express their dependence on God, their gratitude to God for past and present provision, and their confidence that God will continue providing for them in the future.

1. When was the last time you were moved to deep conviction by a passage in the Bible? Do you remember the passage? The circumstances?

_____

_____

_____

_____

_____

2. What are some of your favorite ways to celebrate?

_____

_____

_____

_____

_____

3. How do you cultivate "the joy of the LORD" in your life on a regular basis?

_____

_____

_____

_____

_____

Conviction, Celebration, and Worship

4. Who in your world helps you rejoice? Who in your world discourages your joy?

_____

_____

_____

_____

_____

5. The author suggests that there is a strong relationship between mourning and joy in Scripture and in life. Do you agree? Why or why not?

_____

_____

_____

_____

_____

6. How do you feel about praying prayers of lament to God? What are the hardest words you have ever said to God?

_____

_____

_____

_____

_____

7. What is one relationship, issue, or occurrence in your life or the world that is causing lament in your heart?

_____

_____

_____

_____

_____

8. The Festival of Tabernacles was a renewed way the people began to worship God after hearing the Law. What new practices of devotion to God have you implemented in your life through hearing or reading the word of God?

_____

_____

_____

_____

_____

9. What spiritual festivals or traditions do you celebrate to help you remember the goodness of God? What festivals or traditions does your church celebrate? If you cannot think of one, what kind of gathering could your group develop to celebrate and remember the provision of God in your lives?

_____

_____

_____

_____

_____

10. How does God provide food, water, and other life essentials for you? Describe an occasion when you were especially aware and grateful for God's provision.

_____

_____

_____

_____

_____

11. How is God using you, your church, and/or your class or group to provide for the needs of others? What new ways might God want to use you to provide for the needs of others?

_____

_____

_____

_____

_____

Conviction, Celebration, and Worship

Confession and Covenant

Text: Nehemiah 9

A few years ago, the church I then served as pastor celebrated its 120th anniversary. We had all of the celebrations you would expect: former pastors and staff persons returning to visit, former members returning to celebrate, large meals where laughter dominated the table talk, and community leaders and friends joining us for the celebration. Interestingly, the year before, the community itself celebrated its 120th anniversary. So the community is only one year older than the church. The stories of the community and the church, therefore, are inviolably woven together.

One of the members of that church took a particular interest in the history of the church and the history of the town. A couple of decades ago, he worked with a church committee to craft a 100-year history of the church. He has since updated the documents to include more recent events. Recently, however, he finished a more time-consuming project: he published an official history of the local community from 1893–1950. Up to this point, the story of the community existed only in articles and another small volume published by the ever-active local historical society. This work, however, was monumental for the story of the community. It preserved many items that, without the author's vigilance, faced the real possibility of loss. The church and community are indebted to this gentleman and his helpers for preserving their interconnected stories.

Remembering and retelling the stories of family and community is important. In Nehemiah 9, the religious leaders of Jerusalem restate the story of God's faithfulness to Israel as part of the renewal of their faith commitments. It is in the foundation of God's past faithfulness and their past failures that the people must rebuild their covenant relationship with God.

The setting for the retelling of the story of Israel is critical. The people have gathered together during the same month as the Festival of Tabernacles. The community has invested in a significant season of spiritual renewal. They have celebrated Tabernacles with a zeal and gratitude not seen since the days of Joshua (see Neh 8:17). They have focused on the provision of God, living in booths and remembering God's goodness in providing deliverance from bondage in Egypt and exile in Babylon. They have celebrated God's provision, recalling the food and water God made available to them. The people think of the completion of the temple in the days of Haggai and Zerubbabel, and they celebrate the rebuilding work of Nehemiah, although we must remember that the official story of the wall-rebuilding celebration occurs in Nehemiah 12.

The author here, as noted in session 9 above, is not concerned with the timing of events. Instead, he conveys the intimate relationship between the reemergence of an awareness of God's Law, the renovation of the city, and the renewal of the covenant between God and Israel after the exile. These renovation movements are not three separate actions; rather, they are a part of God accomplishing God's work of return and redemption through the actions of the Persian kings, Ezra, and Nehemiah. Nehemiah 9 depicts a coming of age of the renewal movement in Israel, and this renewal of covenant and worship begins once the people reapply themselves to the sacred commands of festival keeping and worship gathering.

The people of Jerusalem move from the celebration of the Festival of Tabernacles into a time of corporate confession. They gather, clothed in sackcloth and ashes—the garments of brokenness, mourning, and conviction over sin. Sackcloth was the attire fit for only the deepest mourning, when a person or community reached a sadness of the most profound level. Jacob dressed in sackcloth after learning of the alleged death of his son Joseph. David dressed in sackcloth when Nathan confronted him regarding his adultery with Bathsheba and the pronouncement that the son resulting from the affair would die. Mordecai dressed in sackcloth and ashes, wailing and mourning inside the city of Xerxes because Haman had concocted a plan to exterminate the Jewish people. The rough fabric of sackcloth epitomized the brokenness, anguish, and harshness of terrible news and, in many cases, the depiction of a person in deep sorrow over their own sinfulness. The gathering in our text is not a time for celebration; it is a time for fasting, mourning, and pleading for forgiveness. It is time for confession.

Confession is a misunderstood and often ignored spiritual practice in many areas of American church life. Indeed, many followers of Jesus know little about the habit of confession other than the line "forgive our sins" that we tack onto our prayers, the idea of the confessional found in Catholic tradition, or the line pertaining to confession, "forgive us our trespasses," in the Lord's prayer. Seldom do we have times where we "confess our sins to one another" as the book of James commands believers in Jesus to do.

Why is it so difficult for many American Christians to practice confession? First, most of us are extremely uncomfortable sharing our sins and mistakes with other people. Second, we are better at recognizing sins in others than we are at uncovering the sin in our own lives. It is much easier to gossip and complain about the brokenness and missteps of other people or groups than it is to confront our personal sins. At root, this is why confession is difficult for followers of Jesus, whether we are practicing confession in front of others or in personal prayer between ourselves and God: we are terrified of the darkness and sin present within our souls. If we confront our sin, we will have to give up our pretense, superficiality, and impression management and admit that certain sins stalk, tempt, and overwhelm us. Even though we long to become like Jesus, we are not the people we want to be. How can we find relief for this predicament without hiding and pretending?

The answer is confession. Without confession, we are slowly suffocated by our sin, and our hearts grow colder and less forgiving of the sins of others. This has happened to many followers of Jesus, and to our churches as well. Dietrich Bonhoeffer once wrote, "Many Christians are unthinkably horrified when a real sinner is suddenly discovered among the righteous. So we remain alone with our sin, living in lies and hypocrisy. . . . He who is alone with his sins is utterly alone."[15]

Unconfessed sin leaves us hurting and lonely. It leaves us disconnected, not from God's love but from intimate presence with God. Unconfessed sin also leaves us with a higher propensity for judging others harshly. After all, focusing on the sins and shortcomings of others keeps us and others from noticing our loss of temper, words of venom, and lack of love. Without confession, we will not transform into fully devoted followers of Jesus, and over the years our hearts will grow less receptive to the promptings of the Holy Spirit and less able to love others in the midst of their brokenness. In the end, our hearts will turn to stone as we practice superficiality rather than exude the love and grace of Christ. As Bonhoeffer simply stated on another occasion, "Confession is grace."[16]

If confession is so essential to the Christian life, how does one get started? The pattern of the people of Israel in Nehemiah 9 offers excellent counsel in cultivating a discipline of confession. The confession of the people in Nehemiah 9 is both personal and corporate. The people stand in their places and confess their sins and the sins of their ancestors (Neh 9:2). The picture is of people moved to confess their specific sins after hearing the reading of the Book of the Law. The reading of the Law leads to personal confession and personal worship.

The personal confession and worship, however, takes place in the midst of the community of faith. The people are confessing their personal sin, not merely to God and themselves but in the context of a community of sinners who also must fall on their faces before the grace and deliverance of God. From the least to the greatest in Judah, everyone can see others confessing their sins and the sins of their families and ancestors. Deep solidarity and fellowship come from authentic confession among others who desire to follow the commands of God and fall short. In confessing our sins to one another, followers of Jesus claim our shared identity: we are all sinners, and only in the hands of the Risen One are we set free from our brokenness, selfishness, and lack of love.

Of course, few churches practice the confession of individual sin in front of a congregational gathering, Sunday school class, or small group. This is certainly understandable. No one wants everyone in Bible study, worship, or small group meetings to know his intimate sin struggles. At the same time, followers of Jesus miss the full depths of community and fellowship present in the face of real confession. Dallas Willard writes, "Confession alone makes deep fellowship possible, and the lack of it explains much of the superficial quality so commonly found in our church associations."[17] How can followers of Jesus develop a confession discipline that is more than a mechanistic sharing of their specific confessions with God? The purpose is to deepen fellowship and grow a softer heart for others struggling with afflictions.

Two practices are particularly useful. First, in order for confession to take place, one must grow an awareness of his or her sin. This is not done for the purpose of berating or bullying oneself with guilt; rather, it is through examining our hearts with the Spirit of Christ that we discover the places in our attitudes, thoughts, character, and actions that need confession and transformation. There are many obvious sins to identify, but the subtle sins are often more damaging to our souls precisely because we miss them. Developing a confession habit that cleanses us from the mire and filth that is clogging our souls will require what Richard Foster and others throughout the centuries of Christian history have called "the prayer of examen":

> In the examen of our consciousness we are inviting the Lord to search our hearts to the depths. Far from being dreadful, this is the scrutiny of love. We boldly speak the words of the psalmist, "Search me, O God, and know my heart; test me and know my thoughts. See if there is any wicked way in me and lead me to life everlasting." (Psalm 139-23-24) Without apology and without defense we ask to see what is truly in us. It is for our own sake that we ask these things. It is for our good, for our healing, for our happiness.[18]

We engage in the prayer of examen to see what God sees in our hearts so that unhealthy behaviors and sinful patterns are uncovered. When we see our hearts as God sees them, confession is our response, and God's response is grace.

Second, we can develop a pattern of confession with a counselor, pastor, one or two close friends, or a unique small group. These people are the ones you will trust with your broken pieces and from whom you will receive the assurance of God's grace and encouragement to move forward in transformation. These are also the people you will trust to tell you if they see a pattern in your life that is in need of confession. They will do this for you, not in judgment or malice but in the love and fellowship built of Jesus Christ. Admittedly, this is a hard discipline to enact, but it is not without precedent. We have seen how the people in Nehemiah 9 are confessing sin in front of one another, and we also noted above how James urged followers of Jesus to "confess their sins to one another." We can reflect, too, on the work of John Wesley in establishing the rules for his meetings. The following questions were asked among groups of two to three people at every meeting:

1. What known sins have you committed since our last meeting?
2. What temptations have you met with?
3. How were you delivered?
4. What have you thought, said, or done, of which you doubt whether it be sin or not?
5. Have you nothing you desire to keep secret?[19]

These questions probed the heart, and, in the safety of fellowship, members laid down sin and experienced the freedom of the grace of God in community. In American Christianity, this type of confession is difficult to imagine, but when done appropriately it is freeing and loving. In a loving, confessing fellowship, God convicts, restores, and lavishes with grace.

The longest portion of Nehemiah 9 is a communal prayer of remembrance and confession led by the Levites. This prayer is the summary story of the people and their relationship with God over the ages. It tells the faithfulness of God in calling out Abram and in seeing the suffering of the children of Israel in Egypt. It rehearses the drama of God's deliverance of the people from the hand of Pharaoh through the leadership of Moses. The covenant ceremony of Mount Sinai is remembered for giving "regulations and laws that were right and just" (Neh 9:13), and then, the people confess the disobedience of their ancestors in the desert. And so the whole story of Israel is retold, with constant emphasis on the faithful love of God for God's people and on the continuing disobedience of the people of Israel to the covenant commands of God. The final verses conclude with the people assuming responsibility for the punishment of exile and hardship they received:

> You have been just in all that has come upon us, for you have dealt faithfully and we have acted wickedly; our kings, our officials, our priests, and our ancestors have not kept your law or heeded the commandments and the warnings that you gave them. Even in their own kingdom, and in the great goodness you bestowed on them, and in the large and rich land that you set before them, they did not serve you and did not turn from their wicked works. (Neh 9:33-35)

In response to the prayerful retelling of their story, the people make a simple and significant declaration: they commit to a binding agreement and have their leaders attach their seals and signatures. The particulars of this covenant agreement along with the signers are the content of Nehemiah 10; however, the intention of the people is clear. They have confessed their sin and noted the theme of their disobedience to God throughout their history, and, at the end of the story, they respond with a simple, line-in-the-sand commitment: "No more. Our people's story of neglect for and disobedience to God's Law ends now." It is an emphatic commitment and a stake-in-the-ground moment of covenant renewal for the people of God.

We have talked about the power of individual confession, but what happens when a congregation confesses its sins and mistakes to its community? What happens when followers of Jesus confess sins their ancestors committed, in hopes of restoring and renewing relationships with others? What happens when a church takes corporate responsibility for its sin?

A few weeks ago, I read a story in a periodical about a church that had a sixty-year history of emotionally bludgeoning and dismissing pastors.[20] In an effort to re-vision the future of the church, the people came to realize that in order to move forward, they would need to confess the ugliness of past acts. So former pastors and their families were invited back, and, in the context of worship, each pastor and family member received the full confession and apology of the congregation for the actions and ugliness that led to their dismissals. In fact, the pastor of the church even sent out a press release to the community. It was not painless and it was not easy, but confession and repentance led to forgiveness and a fresh start for a dysfunctional congregation. Confession leads to new beginnings by the grace of God.

1. At family reunions and holidays, who tells the stories of the family memories?

_____
_____
_____
_____
_____

2. What makes gatherings with family special? What makes them difficult?

_____
_____
_____
_____
_____

3. Have you ever seen or participated in a conflict at a family gathering? How did the conflict resolve?

_____

_____

_____

_____

_____

4. In Nehemiah 9:5-37, a prayer is offered that traces the spiritual story of the people of Israel. If you wrote your spiritual autobiography, what events would be most important? What people would you include? What lessons would be the most significant?

_____

_____

_____

_____

_____

5. Where do see the themes of confession and grace woven through your faith story? Where do you see confession and grace in your church story?

_____

_____

_____

_____

_____

6. What role does confession play in your personal times of prayer?

_____

_____

_____

_____

_____

7. Describe your own experiences with the "prayer of examen" (you may have called it something different). What would help you practice the "prayer of examen"?

_____

_____

_____

_____

_____

8. What role does confession play in the life of your Sunday school class or small group? In your church worship service?

_____

_____

_____

_____

_____

9. What do you think of the questions asked at John Wesley's meetings? Would you feel comfortable answering these questions in a small group of friends? Why or why not?

_____

_____

_____

_____

_____

10. What corporate confessions does your congregation need to make? Are there corporate confessions the Christian church as a whole needs to make?

_____

_____

_____

_____

_____

Confession and Covenant

Notes

1. Six cities were finalists for the 1996 Summer Olympics bid. Belgrade, Yugoslavia; and Manchester, Great Britain, were the first two cities eliminated in the voting.

2. Quoted in Kathy Lohr, "The Economic Legacy of Atlanta's Olympic Games," *National Public Radio*, 4 August 2011, http://www.npr.org/2011/08/04/138926167/the-economic-legacy-of-atlantas-olympic-games (accessed 12 November 2013).

3. Kelly Shattuck, "7 Startling Facts: An Up Close Look at Church Attendance in America," *Church Leaders Journal*, par. 1-6, http://www.churchleaders.com/pastors/pastor-articles/139575-7-startling-facts-an-up-close-look-at-church-attendance-in-america.html (accessed 18 June 2014).

4. Mark A. Throntvelt, *Ezra-Nehemiah*, Interpretation: A Bible Commentary for Teaching and Preaching, ed. James L. Mays (Louisville: John Knox Press, 1992) 21.

5. Dietrich Bonhoeffer, *Life Together* (New York: Harper and Row, 1956) 82–83.

6. Johnny Pierce, "A Conversation With Stephen Reeves," *Baptists Today*, 21 April 2014, par. 2, http://baptiststoday.org/what-is-advocacy-and-why-should-christians-care-2/ (accessed 20 June 2014).

7. Nelson Mandela, *Long Walk to Freedom* (New York: Little, Brown, and Company, 1994) 368.

8. Patrick Lencioni, *The Five Dysfunctions of a Team* (San Francisco: Jossey-Bass, 2002) 15.

9. A word that refers to people who are unaffiliated with any religious group.

10. Warren G. Bennis and Noel M. Tichy, *Judgment: How Winning Leaders Make Great Calls* (New York: Portfolio Penguin Group, 2007) 4.

11. Mark A. Throntvelt, *Ezra-Nehemiah*, Interpretation: A Bible Commentary for Preaching and Teaching, ed. James L. Mays (Louisville: John Knox Press, 1992) 94.

12. C. S. Lewis, *Letters to Malcolm: Chiefly on Prayer* (San Diego: Harvest, 1964) 92–93.

13. John Ortberg, *The Life You've Always Wanted: Spiritual Disciplines for Ordinary People* (Grand Rapids MI: Zondervan Publishing Company, 2002) 63–64.

14. Alexandre Dumas, *The Count of Monte Cristo*, trans. Robin Buss (1844; repr., New York: Penguin Group, 1996) 1077.

15. Dietrich Bonhoeffer, *Life Together* (New York: Harper and Row, 1956) 110.

16. Dietrich Bonhoeffer, *Spiritual Care*, trans. Jay C. Rochelle (Philadelphia: Fortress Press, 1985) 60.

17. Dallas Willard, *The Spirit of the Disciplines: Understanding How God Changes Lives* (San Francisco: Harper-Collins, 1988) 188.

18. Richard J. Foster, *Prayer: Finding the Heart's True Home* (San Francisco: Harper-Collins, 1992) 29.

19. D. Michael Henderson, *John Wesley's Class Meetings: A Model for Making Disciples* (Naponee IN: Evangel Publishing House, 1997) 118–19.

20. Paul Pastor, "The Widowmaker Repents," *Leadership Journal*, January 2014, par. 4, http://www.christianitytoday.com/le/2014/january/widowmaker-repents.html (accessed 21 June 2014).

Works Cited

Bennis, Warren G., and Noel M. Tichy. *Judgment: How Winning Leaders Make Great Calls.* New York: Portfolio Penguin Group, 2007.

Bonhoeffer, Dietrich. *Life Together.* New York: Harper and Row, 1956.

———. *Spiritual Care.* Translated by Jay C. Rochelle. Philadelphia: Fortress Press, 1985.

Dumas, Alexandre. *The Count of Monte Cristo.* Translated by Robin Buss. 1844. Reprint, New York: Penguin Group, 1996.

Foster, Richard J. *Prayer: Finding the Heart's True Home.* San Francisco: Harper-Collins, 1992.

Henderson, D. Michael. *John Wesley's Class Meetings: a Model for Making Disciples.* Naponee IN: Evangel Publishing House, 1997.

Lencioni, Patrick. *The Five Dysfunctions of a Team.* San Francisco: Jossey-Bass, 2002.

Lewis, C. S. *Letters to Malcolm: Chiefly on Prayer.* San Diego: Harvest Publishing, 1964.

Lohr, Kathy. "The Economic Legacy of Atlanta's Olympic Games." *National Public Radio.* 4 August 2011. http://www.npr.org/2011/08/04/138926167/the-economic-legacy-of-atlantas-olympic-games. Accessed 12 November 2013.

Lupton, Robert D. *Toxic Charity: How Churches and Charities Hurt Those They Help.* New York: Harper-Collins Publishers, 2011.

Mandela, Nelson. *Long Walk to Freedom*. New York: Little, Brown, and Company, 1994.

Mills, Watson E., editor. *Mercer Dictionary of the Bible*. Macon GA: Mercer University Press, 1990.

———— and Richard F. Wilson, editors. *Mercer Commentary on the Bible*. Macon GA: Mercer University Press, 1995.

Newbigin, Lesslie. *The Open Secret: An Introduction to the Theology of Mission*. Grand Rapids MI: Eerdmans, 1995.

Ortberg, John. *The Life You've Always Wanted: Spiritual Disciplines for Ordinary People*. Grand Rapids MI: Zondervan Publishing Company, 2002.

Pastor, Paul. "The Widowmaker Repents." *Leadership Journal*. January 2014. Paragraph 4. http://www.christianitytoday.com/le/2014/january/widowmaker-repents.html. Accessed 21 June 2014.

Peterson, Eugene H. *A Long Obedience in the Same Direction: Discipleship in an Instant Society*. 2nd edition. Downers Grove IL: Intervarsity Press, 2000.

Pierce, Johnny. "A Conversation with Stephen Reeves." *Baptists Today*. 21 April 2014. http://baptiststoday.org/what-is-advocacy-and-why-should-christians-care-2/. Accessed 20 June 2014.

Roxburgh, Alan J., and M. Scott Boren. *Introducing the Missional Church: What It Is, Why It Matters, How to Become One*. Grand Rapids MI: Baker Books, 2009.

Saez, Emmanuel. "Striking It Richer: The Evolutions of Top Incomes in the United States." University of California, Berkley. 3 September 2013. http://eml.berkeley.edu/~saez/saez-UStopincomes-2012.pdf. Accessed 14 June 2014.

Shattuck, Kelly. "7 Startling Facts: An Up Close Look at Church Attendance in America." *Church Leaders Journal*. Paragraphs 1–6. http://www.churchleaders.com/pastors/pastor-articles/139575-7-startling-facts-an-up-close-look-at-church-attendance-in-america.html. Accessed 18 June 2014.

Throntveit, Mark A. *Ezra-Nehemiah*. Interpretation: A Bible Commentary for Preaching and Teaching. Edited by James L. Mays. Louisville: John Knox Press, 1992.

Willard, Dallas. *The Spirit of the Disciplines: Understanding How God Changes Lives*. San Francisco: Harper-Collins, 1988.

Williamson, H. G. M. *Ezra-Nehemiah*. Word Biblical Commentary 16. Edited by David A. Hubbard and Glenn W. Barker. Dallas: Word Books, 1985.

Working for the Few: Political Capture and Economic Inequality. 178 Oxfam Briefing Paper–Summary. Oxfam. 20 January 2014. http://www.oxfam.org/sites/www.oxfam.org/files/bp-working-for-few-political-capture-economic-inequality-200114-summ-en.pdf. Accessed 14 June 2014.

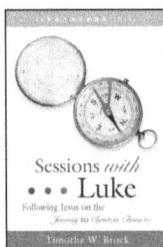

Sessions with Luke
Following Jesus on the Journey to Christian Character
by Timothy W. Brock

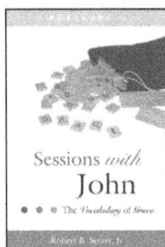

Sessions with John
The Vocabulary of Grace
by Robert B. Setzer, Jr.

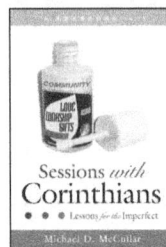

Sessions with Corinthians
Lessons for the Imperfect
by Michael D. McCullar

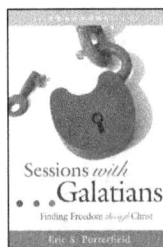

Sessions with Galatians
Finding Freedom through Christ
by Eric S. Porterfield

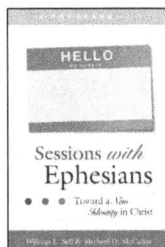

Sessions with Ephesians
Toward a New Identity in Christ
by William L. Self & Michael D. McCullar

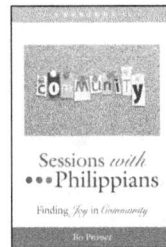

Sessions with Philippians
Finding Joy in Community
by Bo Prosser

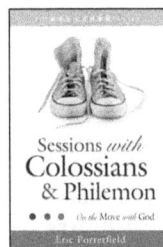

Sessions with Colossians & Philemon
On the Move with God
by Eric Porterfield

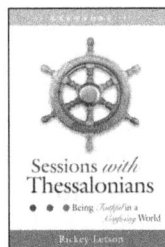

Sessions with Thessalonians
Being Faithful in a Confusing World
by Rickey Letson

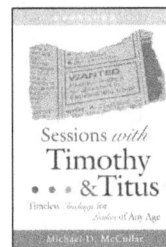

Sessions with Timothy & Titus
Timeless Teachings for Leaders of Any Age
by Michael D. McCullar

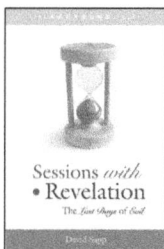

www.ingramcontent.com/pod-product-compliance
Lightning Source LLC
LaVergne TN
LVHW051648080426
835511LV00016B/2559